WE JEWS

Who Are We and
What Should We Do?

RABBI ADIN STEINSALTZ

Translated by Yehuda Hanegbi
and Rebecca Toueg

An Arthur Kurzweil Book

JOSSEY-BASS
A Wiley Imprint
www.josseybass.com

Published by Jossey-Bass

A Wiley Imprint

989 Market Street, San Francisco, CA 94103-1741   www.josseybass.com

Jossey-Bass books and products are available through most bookstores. To contact Jossey-Bass
directly call our Customer Care Department within the U.S. at 800-956-7739, outside the U.S. at
317-572-3986, or fax 317-572-4002.

Jossey-Bass also publishes its books in a variety of electronic formats. Some content that appears in
print may not be available in electronic books.

Library of Congress Cataloging-in-Publication Data

Steinsaltz, Adin.

  We Jews: who are we and what should we do? / Adin Steinsaltz; translated by Yehuda Hanegbi
and Rebecca Toueg.—1st ed.

     p. cm.

"An Arthur Kurzweil book."

  Includes index.

  ISBN 0–7879–7915–5 (alk. paper)

  1. Jews—Identity. 2. Jews—Attitudes. 3. Jews—Social conditions. I. Title.

  DS143.S74 2005

  305.892'4—dc22   2004026724

Printed in the United States of America

FIRST EDITION

HB Printing 10 9 8 7 6 5 4 3 2 1

Contents

Contents

Foreword

We Jews and Rabbi Adin Steinsaltz

We Jews are living in one of the most difficult times in our history. Traumatized by the loss of one third of our population a mere sixty years ago, we frequently hear of Holocaust deniers around the world. And the State of Israel, established in 1948, finds itself surrounded by hostile nations in the Middle East that call for its destruction. Although some find the Jewish people to be remarkable for our ability to survive, and point to our resilience as evidence of the divine spark within us, others are convinced that our long and bitter history reflects just the opposite.

As Mark Twain wrote in his famous essay "Concerning the Jews," published in 1898:

> The Egyptian, the Babylonian, and the Persian rose, filled the planet with sound and splendor, then faded to dream-stuff and passed away; the Greek and the Roman followed, and made a vast noise, and they are gone; other peoples have sprung up and held their torch high for a time, but it burned out, and they sit in twilight now, or have vanished. The Jew saw them all, beat them all, and is now what he

always was, exhibiting no decadence, no infirmities of age, no weakening of his parts, no slowing of his energies, no dulling of his alert and aggressive mind. All things are mortal but the Jew; all other forces pass, but he remains. What is the secret of his immortality?

We Jews are in crisis. Our crisis is both internal and external. On the outside, anti-Semitism once again appears in headlines throughout the world. On the inside, Jewish communities seem as fractured as ever, and our numbers are dwindling. Intermarriage rates are at an all-time high; assimilation is rampant.

We Jews seem to be a complicated bunch. Perhaps Mark Twain said it best when he wrote:

If statistics are right, the Jews constitute but one percent of the human race. It suggests a nebulous dim puff of stardust lost in the blaze of the Milky Way. Properly, the Jew ought hardly to be heard of, but he is heard of, has always been heard of. He is as prominent on the planet as any other people. . . .

We Jews are confused. Our contribution to world culture is well known and disproportionate to our numbers. Yet, for two millennia we have been bitterly oppressed and suppressed.

Once again, Mark Twain describes the situation well when he writes:

[The Jew's] contributions to the world's list of great names in literature, science, art, music, finance, medicine, and abstruse learning are also away out of proportion to the weakness of his numbers. He has made a marvelous fight in this world, in all the ages; and had done it with his hands tied behind him.

We Jews feel vulnerable, but we are confused about our vulnerability. Although it is true that a Jewish homeland exists after many centuries of our living as oppressed strangers and unwelcome foreigners in other lands, Israel is under siege, by hostile neighboring nations and many around the world (not to mention the bitter animosity among various groups of Jews within the State). We Jews have attained prominent positions and occupy influential leadership roles in seemingly all fields of human endeavor, cultural and political. And yet, we know that our similar status in Spain before 1492, like our cultural and societal involvements in pre-Holocaust Germany, were clearly not insurance against the cataclysms that followed.

We Jews are as prone to being stereotyped as ever before. Moreover, the stereotypes remain contradictory. Some call us capitalists; others call us Communists. Some call us internationalists; others call us parochial. Some call us people who keep to ourselves; others accuse us of infiltrating their cultures and lives.

Who are we Jews? Are we different from other people? Why do so many people seem to hate us?

What does it even mean to be a Jew? What do we all have in common? Are some Jews "more Jewish" than others? Why is there so much infighting among the Jewish people?

How shall we respond to anti-Semitism? How do we deal with common stereotypes about us, such as "Jews are rich" or "Jews are too emotional" or "Jews are too intellectual" or "Jews are cheap"?

Who are the recognized leaders among the Jewish people? Who are our authorities? Who, if anybody, speaks for us?

Can we identify values and characteristics that are uniquely "Jewish"? Do Jews have a positive definition of themselves or are we left with no more than the result of dozens of centuries of vicious and often church-sanctioned anti-Semitism?

Do Jews have their own place in the world, a unique mission among the nations?

Is the Jewish people itself a nation? Are we a religion? A race? Or is there some other way to understand us?

Why have so many of the "messiahs" in history, and so many cultural trailblazers, been Jews? Why do so many Jews have a compulsion to "save the world"?

In what way are the Jewish people a "nation of Priests," as the Bible declares? What does it mean to be a priest among the nations?

What are the implications of the uncanny ability that the Jewish people have had throughout human history to mimic the host cultures in which they find themselves?

What is the Jewish relationship to money, a topic that has found its way into both anti-Jewish stereotypes and Jewish self-hatred?

Why has the widely distributed anti-Semitic document the *Protocols of the Elders of Zion* been such a success among the enemies of the Jewish people? Are there any "Elders of Zion"? If so, who are they? If not, what are the implications of this myth?

Why is there a large and disproportionate number of Jews involved with religious cults and new ideologies?

Are the Jewish people a role model for the world or its scapegoat?

Are the Jewish people more intellectual than other people? More emotional?

Are there traits and qualities of the Jewish people that have emerged as dominant over the centuries?

Who are we Jews?

Though there is no official leadership position within the Jewish world and therefore no single individual who is universally recognized as the head of the Jewish people, it can surely be argued that Rabbi Adin Steinsaltz of Jerusalem has emerged as one of the great leaders of world Jewry and possibly its most influential rabbi. In a world where contemporary Jewry is splintered into many groups and subgroups, movements, and denominations, no rabbi is as widely admired and recognized as a true genius, and a spiritual guide of spiritual guides, as is Rabbi Steinsaltz.

This book, *We Jews,* is a work that could therefore be compared to one that the Dalai Lama might write both for and about Tibetan Buddhists or that the Pope might write both for and about Christians. It is indeed a rare and important event when a Jewish leader of the stature, influence, and reputation of Rabbi Adin Steinsaltz decides to address the Jewish people *about itself.*

Rabbi Steinsaltz has achieved, in an astonishingly short time, a unique position of leadership and influence within the contemporary Jewish world, and one that is unparalleled. An Orthodox rabbi, Rabbi Steinsaltz has attracted countless devoted students and admirers in all branches of Jewry. Born into a secular family, he has achieved the almost impossible: his scholarly publications have been recognized as works of brilliance that will stand for centuries, perhaps forever, within Jewish culture. His translation of and comprehensive commentary on the Talmud has been described by many as the most important Talmudic publication in centuries. More Jews today are studying the Talmud than ever before in a single generation, in large part through the efforts of one man, Rabbi Adin Steinsaltz.

It is not surprising that Rabbi Steinsaltz's biography and credits are exceptional. He was born in Jerusalem in 1937. Alongside his Jewish studies and rabbinical ordination, he also studied mathematics and chemistry at the Hebrew University. He established a number of experimental educational institutions and, at the age of 24, he was the youngest school principal in Israel.

In 1965, with the encouragement of then Israeli President Zalman Shazar, Prime Minister Levi Eshkol, and Knesset Chairman Kadish Luz, he founded the Israel Institute for Talmudic

Publications, and since then he has been working on his monumental project of translating and reinterpreting the Talmud. The Steinsaltz edition of the Talmud is almost complete. This new edition of the Talmud has made the Talmud accessible to tens of thousands of Hebrew speakers. In 1989, an English edition of the Steinsaltz Talmud began to be published. Volumes of the Steinsaltz Talmud in French and Russian have also appeared.

Rabbi Steinsaltz's awards, honorary degrees, and scholarly appointments also reflect a man of exceptional ability and demonstrate his unique and far-reaching impact. In 1988, Rabbi Steinsaltz received the Israel Prize—Israel's highest honor. He has been a scholar in residence in many prestigious institutions, including the Institute of Advanced Studies at Princeton, New Jersey, Yale University (where he delivered the illustrious Terry Lectures), the Woodrow Wilson Center in Washington, D.C., Oxford University in England, and the Sorbonne in Paris. He has received honorary Ph.D.s from Yeshiva University, Brandeis University, as well as Bar Ilan University and Ben Gurion University in Israel. He has also received the French Order of Arts and Letters and was nominated for membership in the Russian Academy of Sciences.

In the summer of 1996, Rabbi Steinsaltz's commentary on a classic work of Jewish wisdom, *Pirkei Avot,* was published in Chinese by the Chinese National Academy of Social Sciences. The Rabbi also led seminars at the Universities of Shanghai and Beijing.

To date, Rabbi Steinsaltz has published over sixty books on the Talmud, Jewish mysticism, religious thought, sociology, historical biography, and philosophy. These books have been translated into Russian, English, French, Portuguese, Swedish, Japanese, and Dutch.

Rabbi Steinsaltz has earned a reputation as a profound spiritual leader who does not belong to any social, religious, or political organization. His advice is sought by statesmen and by simple people, and his opinions are frequently aired in the print and elec-

tronic media. Rabbi Steinsaltz has also been invited to meet at the
Vatican in Rome, with the Archbishop of South Africa, as well as
with the Dalai Lama.

It has been said by many who have met Rabbi Steinsaltz that
encountering him is a unique and exceptional experience. Large
numbers of people from all backgrounds have met with the Rabbi
over the years and have come away with the knowledge that there
is something rare and extraordinary about him. After knowing the
Rabbi and observing these encounters for nearly a quarter century,
I believe that I have come to glimpse some aspects of Rabbi Steinsaltz's special nature. One aspect in particular is Rabbi Steinsaltz's
wholeness. When one meets the Rabbi, one gets a deep sense of the
wholeness of his being. He is a scientist and he is a man of God.
He is a rabbi, yet his knowledge seems to span centuries and disci-
plines. He is a man of reason and he is a mystic. He is as interested
in, and eager to explore, the broadest abstractions as he is the
finest, most minute details. He is deadly serious about life and has
an amazing sense of humor.

As stated in a profile published in *Newsweek,* "Jewish lore
is filled with tales of formidable rabbis. Probably none living
today can compare in genius and influence to Adin Steinsaltz,
whose extraordinary gifts as scholar, teacher, scientist, writer,
mystic and social critic have attracted disciples from all factions
of Israeli society."

When one considers the remarkable achievements of Rabbi
Adin Steinsaltz, it is clear that the publication of a book that is
about the Jewish people and for the Jewish people, written by one
of the great Jewish leaders of all time, is a rare and important literary event.

I was offered the privilege of participating in the publication
of this book by working with its author to make sure that certain
points would be clear to the reader. I wondered what qualifications
I had for such an assignment. However, over the past twenty-five

years I have had the good fortune to attend many of Rabbi Stein-saltz's lectures and classes. I have also been reading and studying the Rabbi's books, possibly daily, for as many years. And perhaps most important, I have spent dozens of hours with my teacher over these blessed years, sometimes driving him to his appointments during his visits to New York, sometimes when I have been fortunate enough to have private time with him, and most recently during the times that he and I spent specifically working on this book. It is my sincere and heartfelt hope and prayer that my attempts to learn from and be spiritually nourished by Rabbi Steinsaltz during the past two and a half decades have served both the author and his readers well.

Passaic, New Jersey   *Arthur Kurzweil*
January 2005

Author's Introduction

This is a book about Jews. It is a private, intimate conversation within the Jewish family. It is not that there are dark secrets to be hidden from strangers. Rather, the subjects explored in this book are matters that bother Jews *as Jews*. They are issues that occupy most Jews, especially Jews in the Diaspora.

It is not surprising that these issues and subjects are rarely raised in a straightforward conversation. Sometimes they remain hidden in private thoughts or in deep states of quandary and perplexity. Even in places where the Jews have a clear and firm identity, the encounters by Jews with foreign national identities create an issue that in our day takes on a special meaning. In fact, the modern encounter of the Jewish people with its neighbors is an acute issue, particularly when a large portion of the Jewish people is relatively unfamiliar with its own national self-identity. Too often, Jews get to know their Jewishness only in terms of separateness and feelings of estrangement.

The aim of this book is not to sermonize nor to chastise, nor to serve as an apology. This book is an attempt to see causes and consequences, achievements and failures, and to look at the contemporary world as we, as Jews, observe our dreams and longings.

Since this book is a conversation-like study and a clarification of thoughts that should provoke the reader to further thinking and to drawing his own conclusions, it has not been written as a scientific treatise. Though the facts have been carefully verified, I have dispensed with the academic paraphernalia of notes, sources, and references to parallel studies.

In addition, most of the material in this book deals with Jews in general, not with any particular person, group, or social stratum. It is only in order to offer points of clarification or to avoid abstractions that a number of examples have been presented. Clearly, any attempt to discuss the problems of a whole people cannot be expected to be perfectly accurate. And when one is dealing with the Jewish people, with its many faces, its wide distribution, and its numerous exceptions to all rules, it is impossible to avoid the error of omitting certain important people or events.

There is also no intention here to engage in historical analysis. Though we know that the past is father to the present, and though Jewish events of the near and far past are presented in this book, historical events are not recalled to explain them. Rather, they are mentioned in order to help us understand both what is *now* taking place as well as what we may expect in the future.

Some readers of this book may very well deplore the fact that many of the explorations here seem to be too materialistic and historical. These readers may claim that I fail to relate adequately to certain inner realities and deep religious factors. On the other hand, there will most probably be other readers who will find in this book far too many religious declarations and definitions, and even some that sound mystical. It is often the case that a description of a physical, material phenomenon or even a historical event can express a profound religious truth. Similarly, a seemingly spiritual- or mystical-sounding description of something is written precisely in that way because it is the clearest manner in which to describe or express the phenomenon to be grasped.

This work uses several phrases that may seem unfamiliar to the reader. The words "people of Israel" are a translation of our classic Hebrew name and are used interchangeably with the phrase "the Jewish People." The phrase does not mean the Jewish state, per se, but includes its citizens as part of the larger whole.

I ask the reader's indulgence in having used male pronouns in this book in places where it was not possible to use gender-neutral language. It goes without saying that this small work is meant for both women and men.

This book was conceived in Jerusalem as a result of serious contemplation and in response to meetings with many people. The main part was written at the Woodrow Wilson Institute in Washington, D.C., which offered an agreeable and effective haven for the formulation of the material. Special thanks go to several people who have helped in various ways and at different stages of the book's development including Alan Rinzler, Jeff Burt, Margy Ruth Davis, Ruth Friedman, Malya Kurzweil, Alan Zoldan, Joanne Clapp Fullagar, Judith Abrahms, Paula Goldstein, and Catherine Craddock. I am especially grateful to Arthur Kurzweil for serving as the midwife to this book and for helping me to bring it to light. The final editing was done in Jerusalem, the city where the past always mingles with the present, where the reality of the everyday brushes against the eternal without our being able to separate them.

Chapter I

Are We Actors with Masks?

Our Ability to Assimilate Has Been
Too Effective for Our Own Good

One of the most conspicuous characteristics of the Jews is their innate capacity to imitate, to become a copy, almost completely, of the human environment in which they live. This imitative faculty manifests itself in the most inward expressions of a culture, such as language, ways of thinking, patterns of behavior, and the like, as well as in outer forms of physical type. With the most astonishing aptitude, Jews tend to become natives of a particular place. That is, they more and more resemble the native people of that place—in spite of subtle differences (which the Jews themselves unconsciously learn to detect)—so that they can scarcely be distinguished.

Even in a single generation, this imitative faculty has clearly discernible effects. The children of a second generation of Jewish immigrants to England, France, the United States, and other new lands have been observed to be already so very similar to the inhabitants of these countries that they cannot easily be singled out from those who have been living there for many generations. Not only are their speech, manners, and movements like those of the local people—the very features of their faces change.

Take a look at separated families, whose members have been brought up in different countries. The difference between them is apparent in every way: their movements, their looks, even their physical appearance. Members of the family who went away to another land have become more a part of their new country than of their own family.

One explanation of this extraordinary capacity of Jews to reflect their surroundings may be provided by the existential factors of Jewish life over the centuries. However, a considerable part of the ability to wander from place to place, to live in many countries, is not only a matter of pliability and adaptability. It is also an aptitude for imitation, which, in fact, is shared by any creature that has to defend itself against a hostile environment, whether it is an insect, a fox, or any living creature that is easy prey. The ability to be like the surroundings, to get lost in them, is in many instances a necessity of life, and it has to be learned somehow if there is a wish to survive.

To be sure, this imitative capacity is not peculiar only to the Jews. Various other national entities also have it to a marked degree. At the same time, one should distinguish between a rapid adaptation, which is a mere external copying of manners and customs, and the kind of deeply imitative faculty of the Jews. Certain peoples have indeed shown their talent in this respect to an astonishing degree, not only after generations or years of education, but sometimes in a startlingly short time. Often, however, this quick simulation has a grotesque side to it, being merely external, with all-too-apparent gaps between the real person and the exterior show.

Our Internal Mask

The imitative faculty of the Jews is usually far more profound and, in a certain sense, structurally different. The Jews who try to resemble their host people do not do so only in an exterior fashion; they interiorize this resemblance into their very souls. They not only dress and talk like the people of the land in which they dwell; they think and feel like them.

The difference between these ways of imitation is like that between someone who dresses up in another's clothes and someone who is playing a role. A person can put on any garb—that of a king, a priest, a beggar, or a warrior—and try to duplicate certain aspects of the royalty, splendor, power, or wretchedness of the imagined person. But the whole thing is only a farcical representation; the real person behind the masquerade is quite visible. Whether it is the king disguised as a beggar or the beggar disguised as a king, no matter how clever the clothes or even the appropriate gesture, the personality behind the false front is easily recognized.

In contrast, the actor does not stop at dressing up in a costume; only a bad actor thinks that all he has to do is put a crown on his head and he becomes a king. For the real actor to succeed in his role, he has to do more than put on the right clothes and make the suitable gestures; he has to get inside the role, identify with it, think and feel the part. And the more he can so identify inwardly with the character he is playing, the less he is attached to the outer accoutrements.

∽ A Master Emulator ∾

Thus, the imitative faculty of the Jews is basically an actor's talent. It is, in principle, an inner identification with the outer culture, with all its subtle forms and expressions. This acting by the Jew goes beyond a conscious attempt at imitation. It is as though he himself actually becomes the person. It is no longer a role. He thinks the same thoughts, feels the same feelings, and, when he talks or writes, expresses the genuine contents of the personality he is trying to assume. Therefore, even when the outer change is relatively small (as in cases when the physical features are not so readily altered), the impression given is that of a total resemblance; one can no longer tell the difference between the imitation and the original.

Moreover, in certain respects the actor has an advantage over the original character he is attempting to impersonate. The actor, by his very essence, does not just copy a particular person. He plays a role, acts the part of a certain *type* of individual. When he plays

Hamlet or Othello, he is not imitating anyone in particular. He is trying to identify with the essential quality of a definite role in the drama. Similarly, when a Jew endeavors, for example, to be like an Englishman, he does not copy any particular English person. He tries to get the feel of the essence of an Englishman in general.

Every individual person who lives in a certain culture and environment has, in addition to the general national character, also his own peculiarities, which to a degree diverge from the general norm. Consequently, it is only rarely that he can wholly personify his own national type, because every person has his own manner of thought and behavior, and quite often he even wishes to be different, not to be typical, in order to express his own individuality. The Jew, however, does not imitate the eccentric; he instinctively aspires to the quintessence, the common denominator, and the very root of the national essence with which he is identifying himself.

We Become More Representative Than the Original

It is therefore in no way astonishing that the second-generation Jew, who has become thoroughly integrated into the society to which his parents immigrated, is also, in certain respects, even more typical than the native son. This Jew is more English than the English, more French than the French, and not necessarily because he wishes to demonstrate an excess of patriotism. In contrast to the native-born individual, whose absorption of the collective essence is often partial and shallow and who, in a sense, strives to develop his own private individuality (which may not be identical with the general type), the Jew creates an identification with the archetype itself, which is both beyond and within all the individual representations. Therefore, too, when he shows himself in all his proper clothes and speech, thoughts, and gestures, he will tend to express a certain perfection—sometimes more so than the native-born—of the essence of the local type.

Here, then, is the paradox—that the Jew can be a more complete representative of the national entity into which he has been absorbed than the original inhabitants. It is not a matter of a conscious effort to be better than anyone else (although this too has become an additional feature of the "Jew," who in many times and places has had to make a decided effort to be better in order to be considered equal), but rather that the sincerity of the inner resemblance brings him to a higher degree of perfection. In other words, when the Jew creates in another language and another culture, he will be likely to fashion works of art and authenticity, which express the spirit of the culture more completely than those of the native-born person; whether he becomes an athlete, an artist, a soldier, or a fisherman, he will be that more thoroughly, all because he simply aspires to the essential principle of the culture and does not bother with the side-products or the individual divergences.

Interestingly, it is precisely the Jew's success at looking so completely like the other that is one of the reasons for modern anti-Semitism. As opposed to the anti-Semitism of the Middle Ages and the early part of modern times, which was largely based on the xenophobia that was stimulated by the strangeness of the Jew because he was different, this new form of anti-Semitism draws on the very opposite, the fact that the Jew resembles the native-born too much. A person of another nation may be inclined to feel—whether he expresses it outright or just senses it obscurely—that the Jew has taken something valuable from him. More profound than the argument about the economic or political power of the Jews is the notion that the Jew has stolen the national self, the "I" of a host people. It is as though the shadow not only imitates the movements of the master; he does it so well that the master begins to feel that he himself is becoming a shadow. Ironically, he becomes the shadow of a figure that is only an imitation of him.

We Are Lost in the Role of Our Own Making

This process of resemblance is of course far more complex and intricate than I have intimated. As the years pass, the conscious and unconscious habits become so ingrained that the actor really becomes identified with the role he is playing. But it may take time, sometimes a whole generation. Undoubtedly such efforts to play a part, before the person is able to do it to perfection, arouse a variety of reactions in others, from a cheerful feeling of incongruity, or even the grotesque—like observing a monkey's efforts to imitate one's actions—to a sense of acute discomfort and unease at the sight of someone else copying one's behavior. In any case, it is not a pleasant reaction.

Such unsuccessful efforts to be like the others, bordering on the grotesque, may arouse sour amusement but hardly ever hatred. The incongruity can be despicable, perhaps, but it does not stir a passionate resentment. The imitative facility of the Jew, however, extends so far beyond the external, caricaturish quality of such early efforts that he does indeed become a native, quite indistinguishable as a stranger by any sign whatever. And this is what causes a fierce antagonism among many people. They feel that this stranger has taken their very essence from them. Moreover, the personal enmity becomes a much more general hatred when this Jew ceases to be a particular individual in one's circle and becomes a public image. The writer, the film star, the statesman, and the military commander who are Jews—especially if they are eminently successful—will arouse a deep, resentful hatred, and even fear, because they, even more so, seem to have robbed one of his self-image.

∽ The Spiritual Consequences ∽ of Not Being Authentic

What happens to the actor himself? What about the soul of the all-too-accomplished actor? At the beginning of the period of the Emancipation in the eighteenth and early nineteenth century, there were those who recommended as a solution to the Jewish problem (which was mistakenly seen only as a problem of estrangement from the environment) the formula expressed by the Russian Jewish poet Y. L. Gordon, "to be a person when you go out and a Jew at home." And indeed, many Jews tried, and still try in one way or another, to live accordingly. Outside, in the gentile world, they thoroughly identify with their surroundings, imitating them faithfully, but when they come home to their inner circle of family and friends, they become something else. In such instances, the Jew turns into an actor in the full meaning of the word, acting a role before an audience for certain hours of the day, and then in the "dressing room" changing his clothes and becoming his ordinary self.

This transition puts considerable inner strain on the actor. He has to divide his life into two parts, which basically have no connection between them, his being himself and his acting on the stage of the world. The more skillful the actor, the more he identifies with his role in his imagination, and the more difficult it is to cut himself off from the character he is playing. Even when he manages to remove the external components of dress, speech, and gesture, it is still not at all easy to remove the inner drive that has absorbed his soul in the world of affairs. Even if he does not wish it, he drags his role in the play into his life, and his life is colored, influenced, and changed by it.

The very same element that in a certain respect makes an actor's life (even if not his work) easier is the fact that in general he is playing a role only for a relatively short time—onstage, or while he needs to resemble a certain character. Therefore, it is much easier for him to turn his own personality on and off. But the Jew who acts a role as part of a life environment does not do so only for the few hours' duration of the play; he has to fulfill his social role, with all its implications, for the greater part of his day, and sometimes even for more extended periods. He has to behave this way for years, adapting his acting to conform to changes of age, class, and social situation in general.

Similarly, the actress who is constrained to perform the same role for a long time, let us say that of Cleopatra, has to cope with a real difficulty when she comes home to a baby and a husband. Without question this kind of schizophrenic division, with each segment of life somehow aware of the other, even if vaguely, is a constant hardship for all actors. It is the tragic aspect of the double life of the player.

However, there comes a point at which this person, the Jew who is acting, does not try (at every level of consciousness) to keep his Judaism, when he transfers the character he is playing totally into his life—when he stops remembering that he is only acting a part. It is the point at which his imitative efforts are no longer conscious. The identification with the surrounding society becomes entirely automatic, almost like the reaction systems of various creatures, such as chameleons, whose colors change without their volition, in correspondence to the immediate environment. The assimilated Jew makes a conscious effort to become so absorbed and so much a part of the world around him that he is identified with it.

However, of course, there are also Jews who do not have to make this effort: they are already assimilated. In one way or another, they feel (at least to themselves) that they have never been different, whether they were born into a certain culture or whether they have accepted it with such a completeness that they have lost awareness of any other side of themselves. Nevertheless, for the most part, the process of genuine assimilation takes time and has its own complications. One catches outer manifestations, conscious or unconscious, of Jewishness, even if only in subtle differences. Yet the actor may well have forgotten that he is only an actor playing a role—the role simply takes over and dominates him.

⁓ Who Is Acting? ⁓

What persists in all this role playing is an essential self that is somehow not part of the acting. Beyond the actor there is a person. Sometimes he is quite apparent and conscious, sometimes he exists in repressed concealment, and sometimes he is entirely erased from any level of awareness. This essential self—in terms of the game or the play—becomes the stranger, the other. And this otherness (Jewishness) remains throughout all the degrees of consciousness, even if at times it is on an altogether repressed level. It is an inner essence that endures somehow, no matter how pale and insignificant it may seem.

Thus, the Jew who has arrived, as far as he is concerned, at a complete identification with his surrounding culture will still be "other" at some inaccessible point within himself. In spite of all his efforts, conscious and unconscious, to change and to be someone else, there persists an inexorable, indestructible core of selfhood.

This core may continue to lie dormant for many years, and even for a whole lifetime. And to all intents and purposes, there may be no sign of its presence. Still, its existence does create a difference; the assimilated person is somehow not the same as the others. In spite of all that the Jew may do for the society in which he dwells, in spite of giving all his heart and soul, sacrificing himself endlessly, he nevertheless remains an actor playing a part.

To be sure, he may perform his role with consummate success, with the utmost sincerity, not only because he has to prove himself, but because his urge to imitate is directed to more than any limited individual person or group—it is directed to the spirit of a certain (admired) people or of a (universal) movement. Nevertheless, he cannot eliminate the basic ingredient of his alienation, his otherness. His conscious loyalty is completely given over to the assimilated environment, but the kernel of his being remains obdurately something else: Jewish.

In this sense, he resembles a grafted rosebush that has all the branches, leaves, flowers, and scents of another species grafted onto it. The stem from which all this grows so splendidly really belongs to a different kind of plant, and in its own way tries to manifest itself. Furthermore, since the stem is of a different stock, it can always receive still another grafted plant.

This essential otherness, even if it contains the capacity to be indistinguishable from its surroundings, may itself create a barrier. Because the same individual in another place and other surroundings will again become a copy of an entirely different culture, the very talent of the Jew for imitating one social form can be useful in identifying with another. Ultimately, then, the identification proves to be neither one of free choice nor one of genuine authenticity. The capacity to cast off one form and assume another is not an expression of lack of loyalty; it is, rather, a process that occurs of itself, as with the lizard that changes color without intending to do so, because that is its nature. Nevertheless, it is not to be wondered at that others who possess a fixed color of their own feel that such a creature, who changes color, belongs to a different species.

This measure of alienation—no matter how small—that designates an essential otherness is the factor that makes it possible for Jews to recognize each other within a strange environment and, to a degree, for the other also to pick out the Jew. As Jews try knowingly or unknowingly to identify with their society, there still seems to be a shade of something very subtle and yet very deep, of another essence.

Therefore, too, there is the feeling, nourished by an obscure, undefined, and unverifiable apprehension, that the Jews have something strange and hidden about them. This apprehension is of course another reason for hatred of the Jew, a hatred that has no rational causes and is not the result of the presence of Jews among another people. In fact, the opposite is true. Jews have shown in their lives, as in their dying for their adopted homeland, an extraordinary loyalty. But for all their sincere identification with their surrounding society, there has remained among the people of that society a sense that the Jew, by his very essence, is not "one of us." They feel that somewhere within the Jew there is a strangeness, a kernel that cannot be changed or eradicated.

The assumption about an unchangeable kernel of Jewishness is not necessarily a matter of prejudice or antagonism. On the contrary, it is rooted in the self-recognition of the Jew himself, as expressed by the halachic statement, "Israel, even though it has sinned, remains Israel" (Sanhedrin 44a). It is a basic Jewish mystical axiom (*Tanya*, chapters 14 and 18) that the soul of Israel cannot be completely eliminated, even when a Jewish individual chooses to suppress it and keep it totally hidden away.

The Ironic Tragedy of the Perpetual Actor

The Jews can thus be said to be in this world as a caste of tragic actors. The tragedy of this lies not in the roles they play but in their being actors. The talent for mimicry that the Jew has had to develop in order to survive has become an irresistible compulsion, a need to imitate. On the other hand, this very resemblance to the other, which he so very well succeeds in achieving—whether in his own terms or in terms of the surrounding culture—only makes him someone who is desperately trying to identify himself with his role. His success remains in the realm of art; he achieves only a higher level of the art of acting.

The surrounding culture does not necessarily reject the Jewish actor: it often applauds him and offers him all the material rewards of his success. However, in such a case, the tragedy lingers in the heart of the actor; at some point he knows (or at least obscurely senses) that in spite of his achievements he remains only an actor. At times, when the Jew reaches a broad, more inclusive summation of his life, he can consciously tell himself, as it is written: "They made me the keeper of the vineyards; but my own vineyard I have not kept" (Song of Songs 1:6).

The course of action and the success are all imposed from without—they are basically from some other source, from another personality—while the essential self of the Jew remains bare, stripped of any identity of its own. Ultimately, the basic tragedy is that of someone who all his life strives to be something real and in the end succeeds in being no more than a copy, an imitation. And the more intimately bound the Jew is to the role he plays, the more profound is the tragedy of it. The suicide of many German Jews at the time of Hitler's rise to power was not only a sign of bitterness and despair; it was also a reaction, extreme and terrible, to the tragic revelation of their having mistaken themselves for Germans, realizing that they had always been strangers, actors who had merely been allowed to perform their parts for a while. It is a tragedy that has no solution because it is in the nature of the situation.

The Jew can emerge from it, resolve it, in only one way: when he consciously and deliberately decides to stop acting and to try again to be himself, returning to the original essential design of his own being.

∽ Questions and Answers ∽

Q *How does an assimilated Jew begin to return to his original design?*

Rabbi Adin Steinsaltz (RS) One obvious way is by throwing away the masks, to find out if there is any content left. It's like taking off the wrapping of a giftbox to see if it's just a hoax that has nothing in it. . . . If there is indeed a gift within, then taking off the wrapping will help you find the inner core. That core then has to be nourished.

Q *How can the inner core be nourished? By books? Teachers?*

RS By teachers, by books, by contemplation, by any way that is substantive. Sometimes one finds more questions than answers. But one must try to go to the main question, the main problem, and try to solve it. It may be a question, or it may be like a very small embryo that needs a kind of special treatment in order to grow.

Q *Does the original design have to be religious, or can it be cultural?*

RS Jewish culture is a culture that is religious, focused, demanding, and very directional. Although we are not, in a formal sense, a religion (as discussed in Chapter 3, "Are We a Nation or a Religion?"), our family's culture is, essentially, religious. You cannot become more Jewish by trying to read all the novels written by Jews.

Q *Are you suggesting that the assimilated Jew who wants to dabble in Judaism is really not going to make any significant progress?*

RS If he wants to play with it, it will just be another game. In addition to his Buddhist game, or his poker game, he will also have a Jewish game that won't be more significant than any other.

Q *One can anticipate that many Jews who are interested in discovering their Jewish identities might say, "I want to be Jewish but I don't want any of that religious stuff."*

RS Judaism is "religious stuff." It's not just kneidelach and gefilte fish. If you try to do without the "religious stuff," in the end what you'll have is just manufactured gefilte fish and a fake kneidel.

Chapter II

Are We Shattered into Pieces?

Despite What Anti-Semites Have Said,
Our Infighting and Historical
Circumstances Have Never Allowed
Unity nor a Unified Leadership

In an earlier generation, Jews used to say jokingly that they would sometimes prefer to read anti-Semitic literature, in which they were described as possessing hidden wealth and great power over nations, rather than contemporary Jewish literature, which described their true suffering, poverty, and impotence.

Every once in a while, there appears a book or an article in a journal in which Jews are discussed (whether it is written by a Jew or a gentile) that leaves the reader unsure whether the book is for or against the Jewish people, whether it has anti-Semitic overtones or is altogether friendly.

One example is a book by a French writer titled *Les Juives*, which was received angrily by the Jewish public, especially in France. On the whole, the book is not an indictment; it does not indulge in name-calling. On the contrary, the author endeavors to show that almost every important personage of the last thousand years was either a Jew or of Jewish extraction or at least in some way the student of a Jew. In the book's defense, the author claimed to have written a pro-Jewish book, to raise and enhance the status of the Jewish people. The fact that Jews did not see it this way does not prove anything one way or the other.

One of the most widely known and most destructive anti-Semitic documents in history is the infamous *Protocols of the Elders of Zion*, which represents itself as the Jewish leadership's plan to rule the world. The *Protocols of the Elders of Zion* was known from the very start to be a forgery. It was written at the instigation of the Tsarist government of Russia by a nameless functionary who did not even try to write anything original, but adapted several satirical French pieces that had been written on an entirely different subject. The resulting composition is a poor document, obviously a fake. Most of it was copied from an obscure satire on Napoleon III by Maurice Joly, called *Dialogue aux Enfers entre Montesquieu et Machiavel* (*A Dialogue in Hell Between Montesquieu and Machiavelli*).

Nevertheless, despite the obvious forgery and the shoddy presentation, the *Protocols of the Elders of Zion* managed to spread very quickly after its first appearance in 1872, and to have an influence throughout the world. Anti-Semites everywhere pointed to the *Protocols* as decisive testimony to the great power and destructive intentions of the Jews. And many—thousands, perhaps millions of people—were drawn into this net of persuasion. Even when many of those who referred to the *Protocols* as proof were not really convinced of its authenticity themselves, they continued to disseminate it as an important document for their anti-Semitic cause.

⌒ Do Jews Rule the World? ⌒

Since the composition of the *Protocols,* the situation in the world has altered considerably. Empires have fallen. New political constellations have arisen. Ideologies have flared up and died out. And yet the *Protocols of the Elders of Zion* remains. It has been translated into many different languages and spread throughout the world, most infamously, perhaps, in the United States by Henry Ford in his newspaper, *The Dearborn Independent.* It has appeared where there are many Jews and active anti-Semitic feelings, as well as in places where, for their own political reasons, leaders are interested in fighting the Jewish peril. And what is most astonishing is its publication and distribution in countries where there are no Jews at all and never have been, where Jews are known only as a rumor, as strange people living on the other side of the world. In several Arab countries, the government is itself, officially or semiofficially, involved in the dissemination of the *Protocols of the Elders of Zion* as well as other anti-Semitic propaganda.

There can be no doubt that the *Protocols* makes the Jews a target for enmity and hatred and even fear, and that its circulation is harmful to the Jews in any part of the world. Clearly the Jewish attitude to it could not be other than extreme aversion and disgust. Nevertheless, there is room to inquire whether the *Protocols of the Elders of Zion* (or any similar hate literature) is as thoroughly negative and insulting as it is perhaps intended to be or whether it is actually rather ambivalent in its essence.

Bitter experience and long persecution have often resulted in Jews feeling insulted or threatened by words that were not written with any malicious intent at all and could easily be interpreted very differently indeed. The figure of Shylock in Shakespeare's *Merchant of Venice*, for example, has been a matter for considerable speculation. In certain places (such as Nazi Germany) it served as anti-Semitic propaganda, although its famous author may have had no such intent at all.

Insofar as the *Protocols of the Elders of Zion* is concerned, it is evident that its whole aim and purpose is to stir anti-Semitic feelings, not only describing as it does the power and control of the Jews, but also seeking to show that the Jewish leadership has secret destructive intentions against the order of society. Nevertheless, it is not at all so plain to everyone, and not every reader of the *Protocols* will necessarily reach the same negative conclusions.

A comic illustration of this is the story of a visitor to Israel from Japan (a country which has had practically no contact at all with Jews, either culturally or ethnically, and where the *Protocols of the Elders of Zion* has come out in a variety of fragmented versions). This visitor, a literary critic, brought the Prime Minister of Israel a special gift—an ornate copy of the *Protocols* in Japanese. He claimed that even though the *Protocols* was not in the nature of a literary work and not factual description, still, it was a most flattering representation of Jews and their achievements.

In fact, the substantial content of the *Protocols,* and actually of almost all anti-Semitic literature, *is* somewhat ambivalent. In addition to the enormous envy and hatred there is a notion—which is presented as a fact—that the Jews possess such enormous power that they are the secret rulers of the world.

This raises certain essential questions. If, as Jews, we extricate ourselves from the defensive stand against the defamation of Jewish character and the sheer hatred behind it, and try to see the matter from another angle, if we get beyond the lies and the extravagant libel, we come to the conclusion that not only are we not the ruling powers of the world, we do not even get around to ruling our own affairs—because it is a fact that whatever influence the Jews have does not come to any tangible expression in the world.

∼ The Inconsequence of ∼ Wealthy Jews

Fantastic exaggerations about the power of the Jews have been expressed not only in countries where there were Jews of influence and wealth, but even where the Jews were obviously wretched and poor. Of course there are rich Jews as well as poor Jews in certain countries, but there are other minority peoples who are perhaps just as well off, if not better off.

For example, the ethnic group that is, on the average, wealthiest in the United States is the East Indian minority. But neither these people nor the well-to-do Armenian groups are subjected to public interest, even when the facts become known.

There are in our time (as there have been in the past) a certain number of wealthy Jews who have used their economic influence to effect political changes, or at least to exert pressure on political affairs. Nevertheless, on the whole, to the extent that there have been such efforts, most of them were connected with personal business and profit and were an intrinsic part of the political and economic scene of a particular country. There is the historic instance of the Rothschilds' participation in the purchase of Suez Canal bonds for the English government. This had enormous importance for the economic history of the British Empire as well as for the social position of the Rothschild family itself, but it has had practically no effect whatsoever on the development of the Jewish people.

The connection between this sort of concentration of wealth and the situation of the Jews in any part of the world has been most inconsequential. For the most part, to the degree that the wealth of some Jews had some social importance (besides their own enjoyment of it), it was when they used their money and influence for Jewish activities in the community itself, whether to support Torah centers, individuals, or institutions, to further a worthy cause, or to help the poor. Only endeavors of this sort created changes of any significance, positive or negative, for the national welfare. To be sure, some of these wealthy Jews also paid out sums, indirectly, to further certain political interests. But it seems that on the whole the economic power of the Jews was never enough to effect changes on any broad scale.

The Myth That Jews Control Other Fields

Jews are also said to play a significant role in the mass media. True, the percentage of Jews in the field is out of proportion to their percentage in the population, but in this instance, too, their influence is entirely personal and private, as part of the general culture. Their relationship to their Jewishness is almost infinitesimal.

The writers, journalists, script writers, and composers who happen to be Jewish are numerous enough in this field, especially in the Western world. Nevertheless, even though the influence exerted by a few of the chief figures can be considerable, it never leads to anything at all in terms of the Jewish people. These persons may have an important role in the formation of public opinion, whether directly or indirectly, and yet all this potential is entirely kept within the bounds of private actions and personal opinions. They cannot be said to have any common denominator and there is no collaboration or pooling of resources on behalf of the Jewish people.

This is true also of Jews active in other areas where they are prominent, as in science, for example. Some of these people achieve great prominence and may exert considerable influence in a particular field of science, but these advantages, and to a degree whatever power they confer, are also confined to the personal. That is to say, both scientists who happen to be Jewish, who feel their Jewishness as an accident of fate, and scientists who are more conscious of the national identity may equally reach noteworthy attainments, but, even though they can provide other Jews with a certain source of pride, their scientific work is purely objective and cannot be considered to contribute to any national cause.

A new area of Jewish participation is technology-based careers in general. These fields have enormous economic and social effects on the population and are bringing about a veritable second industrial revolution. The presence of relatively many Jews in computer science may be considered significant, but it is a fact that they have no sense of belonging to anything or anyone outside their personal selves. Their work and achievements remain restricted to the individual.

Since the Jewish potential for effective action (even in those areas where Jews do hold some advantageous position) is far smaller than is supposed by others, and is limited to a very restricted range of affairs, and to the personal success or failure of the banker, writer, or scientist, they actually cannot, on their own, make any real changes on a national scale, and certainly not on an international scale.

The conundrum remains: If the economic and social capacity belongs to the Jews (even if it is not nearly what is generally imagined) and the potential for exerting influence is relatively great, it stands to reason that there should be some expression of this in a number of sectors of life. Yet, in spite of this capacity for influence through their financial, social, scientific, and public eminence, the Jews do not use it for general Jewish purposes, even for Jewish personal needs.

We know not only that the Jews do not exert political control in any country besides their own; in fact, we know that they cannot even defend the general interests of Jews in any country of the world. Wherever there is a real Jewish problem on a large scale, whether it is the security of the Jewish state in this generation or the threat to Jewish life in the past generation, or even the existence of impoverished Jewish communities in various parts of the world, the problem is not solved by Jewry itself.

On the whole, such problems get no more attention from world Jewry than a certain amount of organized philanthropy and as much or as little help as can be given through political lobbying.

⌁ The Jews Have No Leadership ⌁

The proverbial power of the Jews is only a theoretical possibility; it is never made manifest. The reason is one of the many facts falsified in the *Protocols of the Elders of Zion:* there are no Elders of

Zion. That is to say, there is no body of leadership that most Jews accept.

The long-lasting tragedy of the Jews is due not only to the suffering and oppression experienced as a result of being at the mercy of far greater powers; it is also connected with the failure of the Jews to create a unified leadership that could bring together whatever force that they did possess and exert a significant counter-force (physical or spiritual).

Even in the time of the Second Temple, the Jews did not have a unified leadership. Not only did they fail to produce a single individual of prominence; there was not even a group of leaders that could exert the political influence needed for historical decisions.

The Hasmonean kings who were the last monarchs of the Jewish Commonwealth were constantly involved in quarrels with the Sanhedrin, as has been shown by the sharp instances of civil wars in the country. Also, it is clear that their authority as leaders was limited to the country itself and was very weak outside, in the Diaspora. Even this authority disappeared completely after the destruction of the Second Temple, with the elimination of a formal center of national leadership.

Since then, there has never been a single body with the authority to act as leaders for the entire Jewish people or for any of its different parts. To be sure, over the centuries, some men and public bodies have exerted decisive influence over parts of the nation. But they could activate only the Jewish population directly under their jurisdiction. Their influence never even extended beyond the limited scope of a specific regional sector to include the whole nation. And even when exercised within a regional sector, Jewish leadership remained limited and usually functioned within undefined and relatively informal frameworks, that is, without any authority over other bodies.

There is no "Rabbi of Rabbis."

The absence of a unified leadership was felt not only in the political, cultural, and economic arenas, but also in the more private areas of life, such as religion. There was no way of determining *halakhah,* ritual laws pertaining to all levels of life, and there certainly was no possibility of deciding anything in terms of ideology or theological issues.

Such broad decisive authority over the entire nation had existed only in the distant past. From the point of view of undisputed halachic authority, the second-century council led by Rabbi Yehuda HaNasi was the last such body able, and allowed, to determine halachic rulings for all the Jewish people. After this, there were other bodies that at times reached positions of halachic significance. Although they had no full formal authority, their decisions often did hold for the nation as a whole. The last person whose authority was recognized by the entire people and whose words were universally respected (even though not always followed) was Rav Hai Gaon. Since his death at the beginning of the eleventh century, there has never been any individual, or even public body, that held such pervasive national authority.

Even though several extraordinary individuals did come into prominence, men whose religious and halachic prestige extended far beyond their specific locales, no one of them ever exercised decisive influence over all of Jewry. Even personalities such as the Rambam, Yosef Karo, or the Ari, each in his own realm of creative action, never achieved influence over all of Jewry in their lifetimes.

Obviously, many ideological and practical decisions holding for all Jews were made over the centuries, yet not a single one was made by any institution or authoritative body. The only way that matters were determined, whether in the realm of *halakhah* or that of theological thinking, was by consensus, a general agreement on the part of the important leaders over a considerable period of time. Often it took tens and even hundreds of years for such a general agreement to crystallize. Thus, generations could pass before such a reliable consensus took a clear shape.

The absence of a central institution in the world for all Jews, whether in the political sense or the religious, was clearly one of the most important elements in the history of modern Jewry. Insofar as issues were decided, it seemed to happen of itself and not as a result of the resolution of any central body. This was true even in the field of religion, where there were no external barriers to making decisions that would be valid for all Jews.

If this was so in the religious life, it was far more evident in all the areas of secular, social, and political life. In these realms, things happened from some inner necessity, as a result of many influences from different directions. Among the factors that determined the manner of such decision making were, naturally, the private opinions of various personalities, except that no single personal opinion ever had any crucial, decisive influence. The final decisions of any great national importance were made only when they were forced by particular conditions.

⟶ Why Jews Fled ⟵

Similarly, the vast Jewish migrations in recent centuries were not the result of any particular resolve or national wish. They were caused by external factors, and private individual decisions only served to carry them out.

The two great migrations of Jews in the past, from Spain and Portugal (1492 and 1498), and the mass migrations of eastern Jewry to the Americas, especially to the United States at the end of the nineteenth century and the beginning of the twentieth, were not planned or considered. The pressure that made Jews leave their homes was external, and their decision was to go somewhere else; it was not directed.

The migration of Jews to America was born of an undefined compulsion, without any guidelines and often in opposition to the local leadership of the communities. Most of the early Jewish immigration to (Palestine) Israel, which was more guided, was also seldom the result of decisions on the part of official bodies.

External pressures and adversity—whether it was the drastic expulsion of Jews from their places (or attempts to bring about their physical annihilation) or a terrible accumulation of economic and social distress—forced the Jews to leave their homes and seek refuge wherever it was offered.

Even decisions concerning far less significant issues, whether formal decisions or responses to oppressive measures on the part of antagonistic governments, were not carried out by organized bodies that represented an entire Jewish public and certainly not the entire nation. All that was done in these areas was done sporadically, by individuals or bodies that represented only small portions of the Jewish people.

Throughout the generations, lobbyists or spokesmen have acted on behalf of certain local communities or, more rarely, of whole national communities of Jews. They used whatever influence they could bring to bear, in the form of gifts, bribes, or economic and political pressures. There were also Jews who, having attained positions of some authority, were able to use their influence to ease the condition of oppressed Jewish communities or to initiate actions that could further Jewish interests. But considered action of a unified Jewish leadership was practically nonexistent for thousands of years.

Why Such a Lack of Leadership?

The fact that the Jewish people has no united leadership is rather astonishing, and is perhaps the reason why those who have no conception of the real situation find it hard to believe. After all, the

Jews have a single religion, and a language of their own, Hebrew, in which at least the leaders could communicate, and in addition they possess a long active tradition of mutual help and of support for their coreligionists, far and near. Why, therefore, could not all these factors coalesce into an effective common leadership?

The simplest and most apparent reason is the Diaspora. Ever since the destruction of the Second Temple, the great majority of the Jewish people have never lived together in one place. Even if we do not count the other scattered Jewish communities of ancient times, there were two great Jewish centers of exile in the Second Temple period: one in Babylonia and the surrounding lands, another in Egypt and the countries of North Africa. There are several ancient traditions of Jewish communities existing in their lands of exile from the time of the end of the First Temple.

Undoubtedly, too, after the destruction of the Second Temple and the adversity of ever-increasing economic and social pressure, many Jewish communities continued to wander from place to place until they were scattered over many parts of the civilized world. The geographic distances themselves prevented the convergence of leadership forces into a single central body.

In addition to the physical distances, there were cultural gaps between Jews living in very different civilizations. In many instances, the governments involved were very suspicious of Jewish relations with communities in rival empires and tried, with varying degrees of success, to sever all such connections.

Besides the separation caused by remoteness and political conditions, additional divisive factors developed over time. In every country, the special circumstances of the environment created their own existential and spiritual responses, and these in turn demanded different organizational and spiritual structures. The conditions of life, the political status of Jews, and their problems in different parts of the world became very dissimilar. What was possible in one country was often quite impossible in another. And problems that were crucial and urgent in one part of an empire seemed altogether unimportant in another.

Even in the times of the Second Temple (when there was a deep emotional connection with the land of Israel as a whole and a religious tie with the Holy Temple in Jerusalem), there nevertheless sprouted up complementary cultural and political centers in a number of places. Each such center grew and developed on its own and (even when they were contemporaries) there was not always sufficient mutual understanding to build any kind of practical system of unified action, most certainly not cultural. The enormous influence of Greek culture on the great Jewish community in Egypt did indeed bring about a decided creative wave of Jewish religious and spiritual thinking. However, this was relatively strange and removed from many of the other Jewish centers. Thus, even in the same generations, there was considerable estrangement among various Jewish societies.

Jewish Infighting Through the Ages

A more profound reason for the inability to form any central body for the people lay in the divisions and antagonisms between the Jews themselves—even from the first generations. The selling of Joseph, which the Midrash considered to be a primal sin of the Children of Israel, and one for which the nation has to atone throughout the generations, is a sort of archetype of the divisions and quarrels among the tribes.

From the time of the Exodus from Egypt until the destruction of the First Temple, there were only a few times (during the lives of Joshua, David, and Solomon) when there was a central unifying government accepted by all the tribes. The divisions, quarrels, and even war between tribes did not end with the period of the Judges. The breach and long dissension between the Kingdoms of Judah and Israel were basically an extension of this tribal war.

The right of the Kingdom of Israel to be separate from the Kingdom of Judah was the reason for many wars between them. Actually, the possibility of having separate and equal king-rulers among the Jews is not opposed to the essence of prophetic and halachic principles (see Kings I, chapter 11). Such division of political authority existed also, many generations afterwards, between the Nasi of the Land of Israel and the Head of the Diaspora (Rosh HaGolah) in Babylonia; both of them were considered valid leaders of all of Jewry.

The personal and political reasons for all this are matters in themselves, but the result was that even in the times when there was a Jewish state with an independent government, there remained several authoritative Jewish bodies functioning side by side, so to speak, but not necessarily in coordination. The Hasmonean King and the Sanhedrin were only rarely able to function together. Even when they did, it was clear that in fact there were two recognized governments, independent of each other and with a certain amount of antagonism between them.

～ The Two Sides of ～
Jewish Individualism

This dissension among integral parts of the people became a precedent for much of Jewish history. What is more, the division of central authority became ever greater with the scattering of Jews farther apart. The divisions grew into deep disagreements and even permanent antagonisms, to no small degree because of Jewish individualism. Just as this quality has its positive aspects, encouraging self-development and self-esteem, it also has its negative side. If each person is so important to himself, it is hard for him to yield to discipline or to act as part of a public entity.

Coordinated action becomes very difficult with each individual striving to achieve his own aims. Even common aims become problematic when each one seeks to accomplish them in his own way. Individualism of this sort is not only a personality characteristic; it is also anchored to a certain extent in the principles and practice of *halakhah* and in the Jewish way of life.

Ever since Moses, there has never been a single person who held undisputed spiritual authority. Even when there was an institution that was central and authoritative on spiritual affairs, such as the Great Sanhedrin or any other such body, it was the authority of the institution or the official body and not the authority of a single person that counted.

Dissension and differences of opinion between members of the Sanhedrin were not only legitimate; they were considered desirable. For example, one of the strictest rulings is the *halakhah* that says that if the members of a high court unanimously agree about the guilt of the accused, the defendant goes free. That is to say, an unquestioning agreement is considered suspect, as having possibly been influenced by strong feelings or by a general hysteria.

Also, in the generations when divergent opinions were brought up for final halachic decision by vote in the highest spiritual institution, and in spite of the fact that anyone who flouted these decisions was subject to official sanctions, there never was any prohibition of free speech. Expression of opinion, even the most divergent, was not only allowed; it was possible to preach it to others.

Of course, opposing schools of thought were not considered desirable, but they were never made illegitimate, and ultimately it was conceded that "both these and these are words of the living

God." To be sure, the goal was always to reach a single genuine halachic conclusion, but the sages left for all time the differences of opinion as they appeared in the Mishnah and the Talmud. This and all the following literature, most of which continued with a pluralistic approach, has certainly enriched the intellectual capacity and the emotional expressiveness of the Jew. On the other hand, it has allowed the proliferation of different attitudes and schools of thought, which create opposing groups and argumentation.

With time, such antagonisms become fixed in life and thought to such a degree that the people can no longer work together effectively. The division begins with trifling differences, grows, and becomes an abysmal gap. It may be said, then, that too much individualism leads to isolation and separation, to dissension, which, even when not stormy, creates discord and barriers that do not permit the formation of unified leadership.

The divisions within the Jewish people resulted in the formation of several centers of national life, each functioning by itself for generations without any coordination with the others. In the distant past, too, there continued to exist—side by side, so to speak—the important centers in Babylonia and in Israel. Each was a great Torah center of learning and culture, and even if they were not actually at variance and constantly disputing with each other, they still never worked together. And not only were there differences between remote countries; also within a single land, where the Jewish population constituted a more or less homogeneous entity, the authority would often be divided among different groups and factions. In Babylonia, for instance, there continued for centuries a deep cleavage between the two great Yeshivot, Sura and Pumbedita. They carried on as separate schools of thought and of practical *halakhah.*

The Talmud itself has pointed out that from the time of Moses until the close of the Talmudic era there were only three people who held a position of both the highest spiritual authority and the highest political power. The very mention of such a fact indicates an acute awareness of the practical impossibility of creating a unified leadership that could determine the affairs of all of Jewry. And naturally, the continued spread of Jewish communities enhanced the natural tendency to division. Not only did the Jewish populations as a whole fail to reach any sort of unity, but the ruptures and schisms in every country deepened.

⌒ The Common Jewish Sin ⌒ of "Causeless Hatred" Among Ourselves

The inability to reach a common stand on an important issue, especially when clear decisions were urgently needed, has thus persisted from Second Temple times to this day. Long ago, the sages blamed the tendency known as *Sin'at Hinam* (causeless hatred), which was expressed in the discord preventing any cooperative action and decision making for the welfare of the Jews as a whole. Through the centuries, this has had many tragic consequences, because although factionalism may be justified or at least tolerated in times of peace, it can be disastrous in times of distress and disaster.

From the perspective of history, we can deplore the dissension and differences of opinion, whose triviality becomes clear against the background of terrible and critical events. For instance, in the Warsaw Ghetto uprising, a desperate minority decided to fight and the various political groups could not choose a unified leadership.

In the recent era, this factionalism has not diminished; it may even have grown somewhat. The irrepressible growth of the *Haskalah* movement of enlightenment, the organization of separate religious frameworks of all kinds, and the various modes of assimilation into the non-Jewish world have all contributed to increased division.

Even the monolithic structure of religious faith and a Jewish way of life, which all through the ages unified the nation, has been shattered into fragments. These fragments themselves keep on splitting apart into factions, into ever smaller fragments. And the leaders of the various factions never seem to agree. Every important problem leads to increasing rupture; there does not seem to be any way of even getting our leaders to sit together.

The reasons for the discord are drawn from a huge variety of serious theological and religious sources, from political and economic interests of genuine urgency, and from personal animosities of long standing, which, irrelevant and pointless as they are, remain factors of importance. Plausible as they may be, all these stubborn reasons for division within the people prevent the possibility of a unified Jewish action that could further the entire national potential.

There can be no doubt that the Jews need a "supreme council of Elders of Zion." Not, of course, to exert any influence in the world, but simply to assure their own existence, for the sake of self-preservation. It is too bad that such a conclave of leaders is no more than an anti-Semitic fabrication.

⁓ Questions and Answers ⁓

Q *What concrete steps can Jews take today to bring about unity among our people?*

Rabbi Adin Steinsaltz (RS) One step is to put things in their right order of importance. Everybody is for unity. That's obvious. But just how important is it? If I don't consider the little divisions of my small synagogue to be of supreme importance, the unity cannot become real.

When the point of unity is not an important one, the result can be war. The American Civil War, for example, was about unity. In the beginning it was not a war about slavery, but a war about unity. An undivided nation was so important as to go to war for it, and to fight your own people for it, and to kill your own people for it. So if unity is important, sometimes you have to fight your own rabbis, to fight your own leaders and many others, in order to push them. You can push toward it. If there is enough push, there will be some results. But it depends very much on how much importance you give to unity.

Q *Do you think there's any basis for hope that there could be a united Jewish leadership?*

RS I know it sounds terribly pessimistic to say that in the past it was only disasters that have had the ability to do it partially—not even completely. Without disasters, the powers of decentralization are too great. Only some kind of outside force can create it. I would like to have such a result coming from the inside, either from the leaders or from the grassroots. But, so far, not much has been done in this direction because for most individuals unity is not a problem. It is a problem only for someone who has an outlook that is bigger than his private life.

Q *Do you think Jews should actively fight against anti-Semitic writings such as the* Protocols, *or is our energy in fighting anti-Semitism misplaced?*

RS We can fight it only indirectly. We cannot fight it directly. We cannot really convince people who are already convinced of the opposite. We can do some general work, such as making certain things impossible to say. We can help to create an environment in which such things are considered more and more shameful. We can make it really politically incorrect to say such things. Now, this is not really a direct fight against any specific kind of statement. It is an indirect way of doing the only thing that can be done with anti-Semitism, which is to try to somehow put it to the side, make it less obvious, make it less pronounced. Then it can eventually die out slowly.

Chapter III

Are We a Nation or a Religion?

Our People Are Not a Religion,
nor a Nation,
nor an Ethnic Group,
nor a Race

The problem of defining who is a Jew returns and stirs up occasional new storms all the time. Nevertheless, in spite of the ferment it creates, this problem is actually secondary and peripheral. It deals only with a relatively unimportant question of definition. Today, the issue of "who is a Jew" is valid only for those who are on the periphery of Judaism, for those about whom there are certain doubts as to their belonging to the people of Israel.

It is also secondary and unimportant in terms of the far more basic problem of Jewish identity. What, after all, *is* the fundamental essence, the basic connection, that determines who or what a Jew is?

The usual definition of a Jew describes merely the most external factors of belonging to the people. The inner essence is seldom discussed. In those instances when the problem of including a person or a group among the Jewish people, or excluding him, *is* discussed, it is always concerning those individuals about whom there is doubt. It never concerns itself with the central body of Jews, whose identity is beyond question.

Whether it is a discussion concerning Jewish origins, marriage, or religious affiliation, the point of departure is the basic reality of an already existing people about whose identity there are no problems or doubts. The fuss and flurry about the problem of "who is a Jew" concerns itself more with the political than the practical.

From the viewpoint of the Jews in the Diaspora, this problem is a projection of the problem of "who is a rabbi," bound up as it is with the question of the legitimacy of different religious movements in Judaism.

From the viewpoint of Israel, its importance is mainly symbolic, because any clear definition may be used to determine the Jewish identity of the state of Israel itself, which, for the time being, remains deliberately undefined and obscure.

⟶ We Have No Obvious ⟵ Common Unifying Factor

Nevertheless, to define who a Jew is may not be all that simple in our time. In the past, and not all that long ago, all Jews belonged to a closely knit group of people who believed in the tenets of Judaism, obeyed its commandments, and lived in its religious fold. Of course, there were always certain small groups of Jews who were on the fringe, considered separate cults or breakaway factions because of their divergent practice of *halakhah* and accepted practice of the faith.

As an example, the relation to the Samaritans was a problem that occupied the leaders of the Jews from biblical times (see II Kings, chapter 17) until the latter era of the Tannaim (about a thousand years). During this period, there were many changes and differences of opinion on the subject. But this remained a peripheral problem; the existence of the Jewish people as such was never a matter for questioning or doubt. This was so in spite of the many differences in the customs and practices of Judaism in the scattered communities. The common unifying factor was so great that there was never any problem about being Jewish in terms of way of life, intellectual outlook, or relationship to the outside world.

In our own time, however, the problem has become acute. Most Jews do not keep the religious commandments. Even when a person is connected with a movement that defines itself as Jewish, that movement does not necessarily try to express itself as a stable and persistent religious continuation of the past. It is obvious that there was a certain break, so that the Jewish continuity does not flow as it should.

I do not want to touch on the question of the legitimacy of different religious movements in our time, nor on the question of whether there is a basis to their claim that they are continuing the "original spirit of Judaism." It is nevertheless clear that the Reform movement, which openly cut connections with the Jewish *halakhah,* and the Conservative movement, which for many years claimed to be continuing and upholding the legitimacy of *halakhah,* consciously introduced essential changes in daily Jewish life and patterns of behavior, as well as in world outlook.

More common than the Reform or Conservative Jews are those who have abandoned all endeavor to keep the commandments or even to maintain a religious faith of any kind. But even those people who are very critical of all such departures, whether they include keeping the *mitzvot* or not, will acknowledge the fact that they are all Jews.

Consequently the question arises: What is the factor that somehow defines and unites all these categories of Jews who no longer believe in the same religious faith? The definition that, for many generations, has been tangible and explicit for the Jews was religious. Even in ancient times, this was the recognized distinguishing mark of Jews, as in the well-known words of Rav Saadia Gaon: "Our people is no nation except for its Torah." That is to say, what connects all Jews is Judaism, the Torah as a way of life. And it is only that which creates the unifying factor for the large diversity of Jews.

⟿ We Are Not a Religion ⟾

However, the definition of Jews as a religious group is problematic. One of the obvious objections, longstanding and most pronounced in our own era, is the fact that a great number of Jews do not consider themselves to belong actively to the Jewish religion; they do not claim to have any religious affiliations at all. Many people who are admittedly children of Jews and who even identify themselves as Jews do not believe in the tenets of Judaism, do not keep the commandments, and are often unaware of what these things are.

The difficulty in reaching a reliable definition of "who is a Jew" is understandably connected with the more basic problem of "what is a Jew." An abstract definition of Judaism that would be both meaningful and inclusive is not at all easy. Such an endeavor, to determine the basic principles of Judaism, has never been able to get very far, not only because the number of such basic principles is so great that they no longer serve to define anything, but also because an abstraction of Judaism cannot demonstrate its singularity.

It is true that Maimonides' thirteen articles of faith do have considerable positive value in this respect and do manage to distinguish the Jewish religion from others. Nevertheless, even these do not provide a conclusive, positive depiction of a Jew. More precisely, if we examine the more abstract principles, these define many frontiers of the Jewish religion but not its essence. And if we insist on finding the principle of faith in the Torah that we possess, then, in fact, all the details of the Torah are brought in. In this case, there is certainly unity, but again it is not an abstract definition.

Not in vain have sages claimed that a genuine definition of Judaism that would be both meaningful and really Jewish was not possible through any listing of a number of principles, but rather required a wide grasp of certain essentials: the acceptance of the Torah and what this involved in terms of the *mitzvot,* the whole structure of *halakhah,* and the study of certain volumes of thought. And yet even such very broad qualifications do not bring us closer to a precise definition.

Even the sages of the Talmud spoke of various such attempts to base the whole Torah on a limited number of principles (e.g., *Shabbat* 31a, *Makot* 24a). But ultimately these principles, no matter how splendid and satisfying they are, cannot define Judaism. Always a significant truth had to be added: that all this referred to matters of religious practice that belonged to a specific kind of Judaism.

In short, there was no way of getting to the essence of Judaism by any abstract definition. Neither a minimalistic religious determination nor general humanistic qualifications had the capacity of defining the specificity of the Jews. Such minimalistic definitions may be valued for all religions or for no religion at all, but they do not really define anything. Therefore, too, the attempt to define the Jews as a religious entity cannot serve its purpose because the more detailed and specific the qualification of the Jewish religion, the less one finds Jews who follow it, while any attempt to define the religion as that which includes all or most of the Jews would be empty of all content, and certainly of "Jewish" content.

The more basic issue here is the question of whether it is possible to call Judaism a religion in the ordinary sense of the word. After all, a religion is not only a system of beliefs and rituals and actions. It is also an expression of, or an endeavor to express, a general truth that is valid for all people. Whether the religious group is engaged in missionary activities to spread its faith or does not bother to do anything of the sort, it still presumes that its own faith contains a truth that is good and true for all people everywhere.

In contrast, Judaism, which never really undertook any missionary activities in an organized fashion, and was not interested in bringing the world into its fold, nevertheless does have a universal message that is valid for all people. Indeed, Judaism feels that its values should be the legacy for all of mankind. But these universal messages are not identical with Judaism. They are called the Seven *Mitzvot* of the Sons of Noah and are only that part of the commandments given to all the peoples of the earth (the Sons of Noah).

It is a minimal Torah, so to speak, to guide the development of the nations of the world to a higher level. That is to say, Judaism is not a religion in the general meaning of the term. It is very specifically and uniquely the religion of the Jews, which means that even the concept of Judaism as a religious entity involves the preexistence of the Jewish people as its bearer and defines the Jews as that group within mankind, that particular human essence, around which, and only with which, the Jewish religion can manifest.

⁓ We Are Not a Race or a Nation ⁓

Attempts to delineate the Jews according to accepted standards have miscarried. It seems that according to the strictest examination of the facts, the Jews do not fit into any of the usual categories of nationhood, neither in the past nor in the present. Obviously, the Jews are not a race or a distinct racial stock; there have been many converts from other peoples, and many offspring from other races have been absorbed into the Jewish people. The idea of a pure Jewish race is altogether a fiction, without factual basis. Even the Nazis, in their own thorough way, failed to find a racial category for the Jews and they had to conclude that the Jews were not a special race.

Just as the Jews cannot be considered a racial entity, they also cannot be classed as a nation in the accepted sense of the term. The fundamental factors—a large group of people living within a certain territory, speaking a single language or at least belonging to a common culture—have never applied to the Jews. From the point of view of territory, ever since the destruction of the Kingdom of Israel, most Jews have not been concentrated in a single region of land, but have been scattered in many diverse places in the world.

As for language, in spite of the fact that Hebrew served the Jews as a holy tongue and was therefore known to almost all the communities, it remained out of reach for most Jews. The spoken language was that of the surrounding society and the communication between Jews from different lands was just as difficult in the past, when they spoke Aramaic or Greek, as in the later generations, when they spoke Arabic or French. In our own time, the knowledge of Hebrew is limited to only a small number of Jews in the Diaspora.

Similarly, in cultural matters, Jews dwelling in different countries were as different as were their cultural environments. A general Jewish culture was restricted only to the realm of religion. And again, in our time, most Jews have not remained connected with this religious culture. They have fragmented memories of a common Jewish heritage, but these not only fail to create anything of much cultural significance; they also have little in common with the cultures of Jews in other lands.

Of course, the Israelis, in terms of language and culture, can be considered a nation. But in trying to find a common denominator for all Jews, it would be hard to consider them a nation. It is therefore no wonder that observers from outside and honest people from within the fold have not been able to accept the idea that there is such a thing as a "Jewish nation."

⟶ **We Are Not an Ethnic Group** ⟵

Even a far less specific definition of the Jews as an ethnic grouping, which may relinquish the political and geographical conditions of nationhood, does not satisfy us conclusively. True, in a
particular country, the Jews can constitute an ethnic minority of
greater or lesser size and distinction. But when they are seen in
their totality and not as a small minority in any country, the
absence of any ethnic unity is all too apparent. They have no
common language, customs, or physical features; their way of life
resembles the surrounding culture and is not the same everywhere; there is nothing that can be called a distinguishable ethnic
entity.

What, for example, is the ethnic connection between the
Yemenite Jew, wherever he may be living, and the German Jew?
No one could presume to see them both as belonging to the same
ethnic grouping.

Attempts to define the Jews according to the accepted
standards have produced alternative descriptions such as: "The
Jews are people with a common history," which, in terms of the
facts, is correct only because it is the common history of two
thousand years ago. But attempts of this kind to build on the
historical ties between people (even if within a much smaller
time span) usually create meaningless national mixtures or dis-
mantle a single national entity into a number of squabbling
national groupings.

Moreover, a historical connection has meaning only to the
extent that it is known and retained. For most Jews, this connection is hardly conscious, not being familiar in more than the most
obscure manner, and if it is not kept alive and constantly replen-
ished, it becomes an abstract concept, without meaning.

An even more vague idea, which is nevertheless heard constantly, is the "common Jewish destiny." The intention is really to

say that the Jews can be defined by their alienation, the enmity or hatred they arouse in the world. Such a concept, which leaves the determination of "who is a Jew" to the anti-Semites of all kinds, can only be rejected on all accounts. Not only is it morally suspect; it also leaves the question open. After all, what is this element that brings down a torrent of hatred on a people? The observation that the Jews are persecuted simply states a fact; it does not explain the essence of being Jewish.

"The House of Israel"

In order to understand this essence of Jewishness, let us return to the more basic definition in the Torah itself. The Bible calls the Jews "the House of Israel" or "the House of Jacob," meaning that the Jews are essentially and principally a family. This family began as the small group of the offspring of Abraham. With natural increase, they became a clan and then a tribe and ultimately a nation.

But in spite of its extraordinary proliferation, this tribe, and eventually the nation, remained what they had always been—a single family. They are not really a religion or a nation; they are a family. The Jews are thus the people who belong to this family of old, the House of Israel. And almost all that they do, in religious matters or in national affairs, or in any other realm of action, is derived from their being members of the one family. The relation between them and others, and even more so, the relation among themselves, the way they see themselves, is basically that of a family. It is from this sense of family that other aspects of their existence function.

The connection of a Jew to his people is not dependent on his being in any particular place or on some religious or cultural tie. It is rather a matter of belonging to a family. This kind of belonging to a family is different from other forms of belonging to a social group. It is not voluntary, being a fact beyond choice that does not necessarily involve anything more than the practical and emotional relations of kinship.

A person need not love or respect the other members of his family. He may distance himself as much as he pleases, and even act against them, but he can never cut the intrinsic bond to them. A Jew does not become a Jew, he is born one; his belonging to the House of Israel makes him a Jew. The acceptance of the Jewish faith, the keeping of the religious *mitzvot,* or any other way of being involved with Jews or Judaism is a matter of choice, and like every such matter of free choice it depends on the personality and the will of the individual, but the belonging itself is not dependent on the personal will.

This grasp of Judaism as a family is not based only on biological grounds. True, the Jews do relate to the patriarchs, Abraham, Isaac, and Jacob, as the fathers, but the Jewish family is not at all the biological progeny of these fathers. First of all, there are other national entities that are traditionally descended from Abraham and Isaac, such as some of the Arabic-speaking peoples and those close to them, who do not consider themselves Jewish in any way whatever. Their biological kinship to the Jews does not imply any other kind of kinship or closeness.

This can also be seen in the halachic ruling of Jewish tradition that makes a clear distinction between someone who is born to a gentile father and a Jewish mother—who is therefore considered a Jew—and someone who is born to a Jewish father and a gentile mother—and is therefore not considered a Jew. That is to say, even in the instance of a similar biological closeness, the blood relationship does not determine Jewishness.

On the other hand, the gentile who converts to Judaism does not only belong to the Jewish religion; he is considered a son of the Jewish people and even a son of the family. This is significantly expressed when the proselyte Jew, born a gentile, says in his prayers, "Our fathers, Abraham, Isaac, and Jacob." His conversion makes him a member of the family.

The Jewish family, the House of Israel, is thus not a family in the biological sense of the word. It is rather a human-spiritual structure in which people are closely connected in ways that are not necessarily those of biological kinship.

This notion of the Jews as a familial hierarchy has a deep theological meaning in Judaism, as when the sages, in commenting on the Bible, say that "your father" is "God" and "your mother" is *Knesset Yisrael* (the House of Israel). It is in such a context that the Jewish person is a child of a certain family. But the original parents of the family are not Abraham and Sarah, or Jacob and Rachel; they are God and *Knesset Yisrael*. God is the father.

The bond between God and *Knesset Yisrael* is expressed throughout the Bible as a marriage bond between man and wife. This idea is given expression hundreds of times, in many poetic forms and in simple prosaic terms. In all of them, the marriage bond between God and the essence of Israel is either implied or taken for granted. As a consequence of these images, the Jewish family became the "children of Israel," the progeny of such a union.

The fact that the Jew was bound to the Divine, as to God, the father, has profound meaning both religiously and emotionally. The Jewish religion as a whole is actually (as expressed so often in the Bible) a relation between father and child. The special obligations of the House of Israel are those of a family fastened to its special bond to God. On the one hand, they are His cherished firstborn, and on the other hand, He judges them more severely precisely because they are His children.

∼ We Are a Family ∼

Judaism is definitely the religion and lifestyle of a Jewish family. Its obligations are not common to all mankind. They are commandments peculiar to this people, *mitzvot* for family remembrances and testimonies to commemorate central family events and to signify their uniqueness. The strict demands made on the people, whether in the rules for personal conduct or for property relations, emphasize their Jewishness as grounds for severity. And should some of them rebel against the father, they do not thereby cease to be sons. The rebellious son, as well as the child who publicly proclaims himself fatherless, who denies the very existence of God, is only displaying defiance.

The son cannot cease to be a son, and the father does not cease to be a father. The sages of the Talmud (*Kiddushin* 12a) have also noted that the Bible indicates that even when the Children of Israel do not do the Divine will and they rebel, they are rebuked as "corrupt children" but they continue to be children of the Lord always. These remarks of the sages simply confirm the essence of the original religious relationship. God is the Father of the Family, the *Paterfamilias* of the House of Jacob, and further He is first and foremost our father and not our ruler or sovereign.

Of course, the Judaic view of God is that He is the King of the Universe, the Lord of all that exists, and He is also called "King of Israel." Nevertheless, fundamentally He is the Father, and His children are always tied to Him by a very personal and special bond, more firmly and obediently than men are tied by any human link of servitude or slavery or citizenship.

The Jewish family hierarchy of father and mother is basically spiritually meaningful. There is a vertical connection to the father, God, and a horizontal connection with the mother, *Knesset Yisrael.* A person cannot be a Jew only through a one-sided connection with God. Anyone who tries to build such a connection, cutting the tie with Israel as a people or the essence of Judaism as *Knesset Yisrael*, cannot be a Jew.

It is as if a person proclaimed that he had a father but denied that he had a mother. It is thus impossible to belong to the Jewish religion without also belonging to the Jewish people. He who extricates himself from the House of Israel both denies the connection with the Jewish people and repudiates any connection with the God of Israel.

On this, Maimonides says, "The one who removes himself from the customs of the community, even though he has not committed a transgression, but has only separated himself from other Jews and does not perform any of the mitzvot, but goes his own way like one of the gentiles, as though he were no longer part of the community—has no portion in the world to come" (*Mishneh Torah* of the Rambam, the Book of Mada, Hilkhot Teshuvah 63, Halakhah 11).

Therefore, we have the oft-used expression, "He left the community and denied that which was principal." Rejection of the Jewish community and denial of God are parallel; both of them repudiate the bond with the Jewish family. On the other hand, the one tie determines and automatically creates the other, and he who is bound to the Jewish religion is thereby a member of the Jewish people, a son of *Knesset Yisrael*.

Such a conception of Judaism as a family is not merely a matter of theology. It also has its clear expression in the Jewish *Halakhah*. The halachic definition of who is a Jew includes anyone who is born of Jewish parents, even if these parents are far removed from Judaism as a way of life. And even if one's own pattern of behavior is totally at odds with Judaism, there is no ritual of initiation or entry into Judaism.

It is wrongly believed by many that circumcision is a boy's entry into Judaism: circumcision is a mitzvah that the parents of a male child have to do to the child on the eighth day after his birth.

And this mitzvah is obligatory for all Jews (unless it involves a danger to life) at any age. Not to perform the mitzvah is a serious offense that invites severe consequences from Heaven (Genesis 14:17), but it does not negate the Jewishness of the child. Since he is born of Jewish parents, he is a Jew, even if he is not circumcised. The error of thinking that a child is made a Jew by circumcision comes from confusing the concepts of circumcising a proselyte to become Jewish and the Christian ritual of baptism of infants.

⤙ Once a Jew, Always a Jew ⤚

Just as there is no ritual of initiation, there is no way of leaving Judaism. Someone who removes himself and converts to another religion (even if it is one that denies Judaism completely) is considered, in terms of *halakhah* at least, a sinner to be despised and hated, and yet he remains a Jew. The halachic ruling maintains that "even if he has sinned—he is still a Jew" (*Sanhedrin* 44a, 46a). Despite all the severe punishments from man and heaven, an apostate cannot be deprived of his Jewishness, neither he nor his natural descendants after him.

In short, the tie with Jewishness is like any other blood tie. It cannot be changed, and a person cannot leave the Jewish family. To be a member of a family is a fact that a person can relate to emotionally in any manner he pleases, but he cannot alter the fact or cut the tie. He is genetically bound up with the family past, and thereby also bound to its present and future.

For the same reason, a person cannot leave or be ejected from the Jewish family. In actuality, as in private families, a person can run away from home and try to forget his origins, or the members of a family may decide to throw out an individual who has disgraced himself. Even if both sides were to sever all connection, whether by word of mouth or by some sort of ceremony and practical excommunication, the essential tie could not be cut.

There is no way of leaving the Children of Israel. A Jew who assumes another religion, and in many matters ceases to have any relation at all with Judaism, is still a Jew. There is no way, not by an individual decision nor by the authority of a social body, to take away anybody's Jewishness. Even the one who is excommunicated is merely being punished and set aside; he is being separated from the community and its benefits; he is not deprived of his identity as a Jew or of his Jewish religious obligations.

The same is true for those who enter the Jewish fold by conversion. The *Halakhah* expresses this "family" connection by identifying the act of joining the religion with a tie to the Jewish people. It is a family tie. A proselyte Jew is like a newborn babe (*Yevamot* 27a). The entry into Judaism is an extrication from previous biological antecedents and a rebirth as a child of the family of Israel.

Although converts can choose any personal name they wish, their father's name is always *Avraham Avinu* (our father Abraham) and their mother's name is *Sarah Imeinu* (our mother Sarah). Even though they are perhaps not a direct descendant of these archetypal parents, they are nevertheless a son or daughter of the family tree; the conversion is a process of adoption into the "tribe" and they becomes the rightful progeny of the common patriarch and matriarch. From that hour they are part of all that the Torah delineates as "your brother" or "your sister" for all of Israel. They are also Jews in the sense that they cannot leave the fold even if they so wish; if they abandon Judaism altogether, they remain Jews according to the *Halakhah,* "Jews who have sinned."

From this point of view, we may see why Judaism does not have missionary inclinations to bring other people into the fold. Over the centuries, there have surely been attempts to proselytize, either by forced conversion, like the mission of the Hasmonean king Jonathan to convert the Edomites, or by persuasion, like the efforts of the Kuzari emissaries in Russia. However, these attempts were not made with any halachic sanction; they were driven primarily by political motives and not religious ones.

Voluntary societies of all sorts can grow in numbers by conscripting new members. A family, however, cannot go out into the street looking for candidates to be lured or dragged into the clan. If someone should somehow enter the family, he is received with due propriety, but the Jewish family, even if it is proud of itself and anxious about the loss of members, does not go looking for new relatives. The attitude toward the religion, accordingly, is that Judaism is the religion of the Jews; it is their own style of life and worship.

Judaism as a family religion is thus not a matter of theology or *Halakhah*. It is a certain basic essence that comes to social expression in terms of the relationship of Jews with each other and with others and in terms of existential feeling. Even the attitudes of other peoples, which may not reach such a clear definition of the Jewish essence, also feel and express this peculiar quality. No matter how the individual Jew behaves and no matter how thorough his assimilation into the surrounding society, he remains a Jew in the eyes of the others, just as he will remain a member of his family in spite of any circumstance he may have brought on himself or had forced on him.

⟶ Assimilation Is Never Complete ⟵

Often enough, the non-Jewish society will receive the Jew with open arms, ignoring, for whatever reason, his previous family connections. But they cannot forget them. The feeling that the Jew is somehow or other a stranger, a son of a different family, does not necessarily breed hatred. Other peoples can relate to Jews, as individuals or as a group, with a certain sincere regard, even esteem, but they generally do so as to another family.

Even if a Jewish individual comes close to non-Jewish society culturally and religiously and also belongs to the same national sector and talks the same way, he nevertheless remains a member of another family, the House of Jacob. Even if he himself does not feel any Jewish connection and tends rather to dislike Jews, the others cannot see him as something separate from his family of origin. No matter whether Jews are accepted or rejected for being what they are, or whether they are treated with a certain abysmal indifference, past a certain point the Jewish person remains a Jew forever.

The clan-like nature of the Jewish connection is expressed most emphatically in Jewish life and Jewish customs. It is so in those sectors of the nation that are fully conscious of the Jewish heritage in clear-cut theological and halachic terms, as well as in those segments of Jewry whose forms of life and national feeling are not clearly conscious of this.

The basic feeling that Judaism is a family connection also works upward, in terms of a parent-child relation to God, with the national-religious essence felt as an inner family relation that is not the province of abstract theology or political definition. It is no less so in the horizontal connection within the Jewish community, which remains that of the members of the family.

This basic feeling explains, on the one hand, the great intimacy of the Jewish tie, the very real feeling of brotherhood between Jews even when they have nothing much in common. That which is written "We are brothers, sons of the one man" (Genesis 42:12) has been used by Jews of all generations in all lands, in spite of huge differences between them. It expresses the blood kinship of a brotherhood that goes beyond space and familiarity and common destiny.

This strong sense of kinship also explains another aspect, not necessarily praiseworthy, of Jewish life. The Jewish family, like all families, has its own measure of conflict and disharmony. We may even presume that precisely this intimacy and warmth create an enormous amount of contention and quarrelsomeness, maybe even more than among other people.

⌒ We Treat Each Other Like a Family ⌒

Internal squabbling within a family is probably more common than disputes with outsiders and can reach a high degree of tension and hatred. The closeness of people may itself be the cause of constant strife, especially when, as in a family, the participants cannot separate. True, a certain physical space can be put between the members of a family, but they cannot alter the fundamental bonds between them.

An essential quarrel between members of a family cannot be resolved in the same matter-of-fact fashion as one between unrelated persons, whose differences of opinion or antagonism of interests can be brought to an end simply by saying, "Let's part and stop bothering each other." In such a manner, open war can be averted, but for members of a family, the problem persists and is not resolved. Out of a feeling of closeness and family obligation, every member of a family feels responsible for the others, and when they do something he considers wrong, he feels obligated to interfere and set them right.

Two strangers find it much easier to agree that they disagree; two kinsmen find it almost impossible, because the very possibility of distancing oneself from others, from their laws and customs and the clannish unity of the family, is something the family cannot accept. Quarrels can continue endlessly but separation cannot be countenanced. Even when the situation becomes intolerable in practical terms, and the resentment and dislike reach a point at which it is necessary to effect a physical parting between the antagonists, there persists nevertheless a feeling of responsibility for the other; in spite of what I think, the other remains my kinsman, my brother. And whatever he does is somehow, after all, connected with me.

Another aspect of Jewish interrelationships that is typical of a family is the freedom to say awful things to each other in the heat of contention—the shadow of intimacy. Indeed, such family quarrels are soon forgotten. However, as a child might explain it, I am allowed to fight with my kid brother and beat him up, but woe to anyone else who does so.

Whenever there is a threat from outside, the Jewish family reacts as a united body. It is not necessarily a rational response to attack. Often it would be more convenient and logical for an individual Jew or the people as a whole to pay no attention to a Jewish troublemaker. But that is simply not done. There is no clear reasoning involved. A Jew is inwardly compelled to come to the defense of a fellow Jew by a family feeling that may be well hidden from his own awareness.

This profound sense of kinship may also explain the dramatically unpredictable responses of many persons who all their lives were far removed from anything Jewish, and yet when pressed by outer forces to forego this connection with Jewishness, refused, and were prepared to pay the utmost penalty. The list of Jewish martyrs throughout the ages includes not only saints who sacrificed their lives for God, but also people of much lesser stature, individuals who were far removed from religion or Jewish consciousness.

Evidently, the ordinary definitions of a religion or a nation do not fit the Jews. Nevertheless, when the Jews are seen as an enlarged family or clan, their essence and way of life become aspects of the relationship of Jews as individuals to their family. The religion and faith are part of the rational and emotional tie between "children" and their father. The patterns of behavior and of life are the family way of the ancestors, and the national connection is only an extension of this family bond. It is a family that grew over the generations until it became a nation and yet remained in essence a family.

This is perhaps the unique quality of the Jewish connection. Sociologically, the family is the elemental unit of humanity. It is in many ways the most primal and primitive of social bonds, in contrast to national loyalty and belonging to a religious community, relatively modern and sophisticated connections. National, cultural, and religious ties are rational and conscious.

Family ties, however, are obscure and profound and far more difficult to articulate. But it is this very depth of experience that may have secured Jewish existence. It may be seen as a primitive and emotionally charged quality in the human soul, and not to be explained. It is, nevertheless, inexorably real and enduring.

⁓ Questions and Answers ⁓

Q *If Jews are a family, what is the basis of conversion?*

Rabbi Adin Steinsaltz (RS) The notion of conversion is socially, culturally, and theologically considered an adoption. A person who is converted is adopted into the family. Therefore, like any adopted child, he calls his adoptive parents Father and Mother.

Q *So the basis of conversion is not an idea that somehow a Jewish soul ended up in the wrong body?*

RS That may be a theological explanation. There is also the notion that when, as it is said, the Almighty offered the Torah to the nations and only the Children of Israel accepted it, there must have been some members of the other nations ready to accept the Torah. Converts may be the souls of those nations that were ready to accept the Torah. But when you deal with it in a more concrete way, it is not mystical; basically it is a ceremony of adoption. The convert is getting into the family, not only getting into the religion. Nobody can get into the Jewish religion without getting into the family, so it's an adoption. Halachically as well, the proselyte, when he prays, speaks about the God of our fathers Abraham, Isaac, and Jacob.

Q *If we Jews are a family, are we a dysfunctional family?*

RS I'm not sure. In many ways, we are functioning like a very normal family, not an ideal family. We are a normal family, which means a fair amount of infighting, of disputes. In a normal family when any member is in trouble he is automatically helped. If a member is attacked, the family will come to his defense, again automatically, without thinking. Later on, they may settle their accounts. It doesn't mean that everything becomes peaceful. In that sense, in many ways we are still functioning as a family. As I say, a very normal family, which means lots of fights, lots of bickering. Sometimes when you become an adult, the bickering becomes less acrimonious; at least the members don't hit each other. But that's it, that's a family. A functional family is not only sweetness and light, just as a functional husband and wife are not always love and kisses.

Chapter IV

Do We Have Our Own Set of Character Traits?

Yes, But Sometimes We Use Them and Sometimes We Abuse Them

In order to address the question "Do we have our own set of character traits?" it is first essential to discuss the demographic status of our community and the way it has evolved over the centuries.

The number of Jews in the world today is approximately fifteen million. The exact number cannot be measured because most of the countries in the world do not have any instituted and verifiable statistics for the number of Jews. Furthermore, the number also depends on different definitions of the terms *Jewish* and *non-Jewish*. Therefore, the numbers are not exact, and according to various definitions and other circumstances, the number of Jews may be larger or smaller, so we have only an approximate number.

In our time, this number is said to be about three-thousandths of a percent (.003%) of the entire world population. However, if we calculated the number of people who *should* be included in a count of the Jewish people, we would probably arrive at very different numbers.

∼ A Demographic Mystery ∼

Although we do not have tested data, according to the estimate of many scholars, the number of Jews in the world at the beginning of the Christian era was about five million. Correspondingly, it is estimated that the number of Chinese at that time was nearly 40 million. In the course of the two millennia that have passed since then, the number of Chinese has reached nearly a billion, which is twenty-five times more. On the other hand, the number of Jews in the world has increased only threefold. If the increase in the number of Jews had corresponded to that of other nations, the number of Jews would now be more than 200 million.

The question arises: What happened to all those missing Jews? How did this huge number of people who should have, demographically, been part of the Jewish people disappear? Over the generations there were, of course, wars and natural disasters that reduced the number of people. But this does not explain these large differences. Such wars and natural disasters befell other people as well, and in every calculation of natural increase that we make, we take into account all these occurrences, diseases, and other factors that lower the numbers.

Of course, the Jewish people have suffered in a particular way from deliberate campaigns of destruction, from the wars of Bar Kokhba until our own time. But on the other hand, the Jewish people have also had many advantages with regard to their physical existence. Their exiled state, in spite of its inherent difficulties, provided the Jews with the possibility—which most inhabitants of other countries did not have—of wandering and migrating from place to place. Moreover, it also gave them a certain kind of flexibility and made them capable of adapting to new conditions, as other people could not. For example, nations that were composed mainly of farmers bound to their land were extremely vulnerable to every natural disaster that befell them, whereas the Jews were not affected by such catastrophes.

Furthermore—as can be seen from descriptions and accounts of the nineteenth century and even before it—the Jews had a great advantage over other nations with regard to their birthrate. In addition to the special commandment placed upon the Jews to be fruitful and multiply, because of which the Jews did not try, or tried only to a very small extent, to limit the birthrate, the Jewish people have always taken good care of their children and tried to protect them from harm more than other people did.

To this should be added the greater care given to personal hygiene that apparently caused the number of Jews who succumbed to the Black Death and other epidemics in Europe to be much smaller than the number of those among the general population who died of the plague. Another factor was the well-developed system of mutual assistance that existed among Jewish people, which allowed those who had become impoverished to recover and be rehabilitated, or at least not to die of starvation. For all these reasons, it appears that the life expectancy of every Jew was no less, and perhaps greater, than that of a member of any other nation in corresponding periods of time.

An example of the enormous birthrate potential of the Jewish people can be seen in what took place in the 250 years between the period in which it reached its lowest population at the end of the seventeenth century, when the number of Jews in the world was estimated to be less than a million, and the beginning of the twentieth century, at the time of the First World War, when there were between 18 million and 19 million Jews in the world.

The Reasons for Our Negligible Population Growth

According to all these calculations from the beginning of Jewish existence about three thousand years ago until today, it is clear that had the natural increase and existence of the Jews progressed normally, the number of Jews in the world would have been enormous. For this reason, the fact that the number of Jews in our time is so small is evidence of the existence of other processes that act against natural increase and also against the addition—which in certain generations was more significant—of converts from other nations.

This means that there exists in the Jewish people a very severe and serious process of thinning out, a process that transmits only a small number of people from one generation to another. There are, of course, periods of rising and falling, but the fact that the numbers are always found to be within stringent limitations indicates that there are processes that cause the restriction of the Jewish people to small numbers.

The processes that cause the diminution of the number of Jews in the world are a complex series of enormous external pressures, and to some extent also of internal pressures, that result in making a large number of people, who by origin should have belonged at some period to the Jewish people, no longer part of it. These processes, which are basically voluntary, not random, create a certain character, certain traits. This means that all those families or individuals who could not face the external and internal choices opted out either from the world in general or from the Jewish national and religious framework.

The external pressures are known and notorious. The status of Jews for many generations was that of an exiled people. It should be remembered that for more than 2,500 years a large portion of the Jewish people—generally the majority—no longer lived in its own land, but was in exile. Actually, it may be said that this process began even earlier, with the continuous exile of the ten tribes to various places that led to their total or nearly total loss. The existence of a people in exile is necessarily much more feeble and frail than the existence of a people in its own land. Every national or religious minority, even when there is no discrimination against it at all, is in a position inferior to that of the ruling majority, both in its ability to retain the resources that enable it to function normally and in its ability to guard against injury and harm, either internal injuries such as rebellions, riots, or civil wars, or external attacks.

Furthermore, for religious reasons, in most generations the Jewish minority did not often have the same status as other minorities. In the best instances, it existed as a tolerated minority, but in most generations it was consistently persecuted by the majority, and was subjected to very heavy pressure both in relation to its economic status and also for its very existence as a people. In most places of their exile, the Jews were an ethnic minority and also a religious one.

Moreover, in most places and periods of time the Jewish religion was not only different from, but stood in unbridgeable opposition to, the religions of the ruling nations. In fact, unlike most of the many minorities in the Hellenistic, Roman, and other kingdoms, the Jews were unable to create a syncretistic religious system because the very acceptance of such a system would be the negation of Judaism.

These difficulties, which were the fate of the Jews even in the polytheistic societies of Greece, Rome, Babylon, and Persia, became much worse under the rule of the two other monotheistic faiths, Christianity and Islam. It is just because these two religious faiths drew their nourishment from the Jewish religion that they sometimes have a deep inward inability to accept the existence of the Jews and to consent to it. The persecution of the Jews thus becomes not only an expression of hatred toward the foreigner, of simple xenophobia, but also something that actually depends on and is conditioned by the religious system of the ruling nations.

Pressure, both internal and external, varied with time and place, from periods of relative calm, in which there was only moderate pressure, to periods of crusading massacres in which the Jews were violently compelled to undergo conversion. Sometimes the Jews were given the choice of leaving all their possessions behind and departing without anything, but sometimes they were not even given this choice, and the only one they had was to convert or die.

Jewish history has, for generations, told the stories of heroism and martyrdom, and of the daily courage of existence under pressure, persecution, and repeated banishments. Yet there are no such stories about those people who could not withstand these pressures, including those who simply could not continue to maintain their existence—those who died of starvation, of distress, of the hardships of exile, of murders and the like, and those who converted and became assimilated to the ruling majority until time left no trace of them.

⌒ A Process of Social Selection ⌒

But the pressures and difficulties of Jewish existence were not only external ones. Some of them were undoubtedly also internal pressures—the difficulties that result from the Jewish existence *per se*. Observing the commandments imposes many daily and never-ending duties on the Jew. The fact is that even during those years when the people of Israel was still living in its land, these pressures and difficulties of Jewish existence already prevailed, making enormous demands on every person: obeying the commandments, contributing a large portion of one's income to various religious needs, a perception of faith that was not easy or simple, and—no less than all this—the special duty to be learned and conversant with Jewish customs and traditions. Whoever was unable to face these difficulties could either opt out of the Jewish community voluntarily or find refuge from it in some way.

All these difficulties, both internal and external, create a continuous and endless process of making choices. The process results in only a small number of people able to face all the pressures and continue to exist in general, and to remain part of the Jewish people in particular. As a reminder of this, one might even consider the Patriarchs, since only one of the many sons of Abraham continued in his path, while each of the others went his own way without any connection to continuing in the tradition. And it was the same with Isaac. Although he had two sons, his descendants are divided between the children of Jacob, who continue in his path and the sons of Esau, who went off into another kind of world, another path, indifferent and even hostile.

This development, even though in some generations it was more moderate and in others more severe, works entirely in one direction. Although this direction creates, on the one hand, a constant thinning out of the Jewish people, in every process of choice it also creates something else: a certain character, a certain type of people who have undergone these processes of choice and continue to be loyal because they possess within them a combination of qualities that allows them to withstand such difficulties, and also to transmit the message to their children.

We Have Been Strengthened by Adversity

A number of such generations—over a hundred that followed each other in succession—have undergone the same process of choice, enough to build up a certain character, even externally, just as the cultivators of plants or animals might do with the plants and animals in their care. This process of choice created certain character traits in the Jewish people, ways of thinking and behavior, which are typical and characteristic of those who have undergone this great course of selection.

Moreover, throughout the generations, the Jewish people have also taken in converts who underwent these processes of choice. And since these processes are not essentially defined by certain conditions or external traits, it is clear that they are mainly a matter of character, of mental qualities. Standing behind each Jew are many generations of those who have also had the will and ability to continue in this particular path, and therefore it is clear that these acquired qualities are not only those of the individual, but have been inherited and cannot easily be dispensed with.

Of course, every Jew always has the choice of whether or not to stay "inside," and this free choice exists today just as it did in the past. Yet this does not imply that one can leave behind the inner qualities that belong to the essential Jewish nature. These qualities, which were formed and fashioned over so many generations, created a certain type of person who cannot extricate himself from his heritage by personal decision. A personal decision can change his place in society, but it cannot change his character and mental qualities. These remain wherever a Jew may be found, in every walk of life, nation, or ideology that he might choose for himself.

As we have said, the Jewish qualities are linked only in part to the essential aspects of Judaism, while partially deriving from the series of choices and alternatives that presented themselves over the generations. These qualities are of many different kinds, and certainly it is impossible to list all of them together, or even to arrange them according to any defined order of importance. Moreover, as with every assemblage of character traits, certain aspects are more prominent and recognizable in certain people and are almost absent in others. Also, external conditions undoubtedly have considerable influence over the possession and appearance of specific character traits. There are conditions under which certain qualities, which are usually hidden or nearly invisible, find expression, whereas other conditions do not demand them and do not even allow them to be revealed.

Our Flexibility Is a Critical Survival Skill

Among these qualities one may list a very high survival capability, which includes the ability to adapt oneself to many and varied situations, even the most severe and difficult ones. Some of the important elements that are deeply rooted in the Jewish faith are the will to live and the belief in life, including even life under the most difficult conditions. But this will is also accompanied by many talents that assist in survival, including great flexibility—that is, the ability to change situations, ways of life, languages, and the like, without remaining too attached to older structural patterns.

As we have said, the Jew also has an enormous talent for imitation and simulation, externally and internally, of the surrounding environment, because of the frequent need—sometimes out of choice, but generally produced by force—to leave one place for another. Those who remain closely attached to a certain fixed pattern cannot survive in a new place and under different conditions. Even when one lives in a ghetto, in order to live within a certain society he must not only adapt himself to outward manners, but to a great extent he must have the inward ability to identify himself with the surrounding society. Only then can he live within it, even if he is an unwanted stranger to it.

This flexibility and survival capability includes the ability to wander, to journey from one place to another. Although the Jews, unlike the gypsies, for example, have never based their way of life on nomadic migration, and to a great extent have done their best to maintain a hold on their places of residence, this hold was nevertheless—either consciously or unconsciously—only a partial one. This was mainly caused by the constant expulsions and pressures, which were sometimes unbearable, but no less so by the definition, which was made nearly everywhere, of the Jews as aliens.

This definition is not only a legally valid one; it is also internalized, because when people are told that they are foreigners—whether persecuted or tolerated—they must also see themselves to some degree as foreigners. On the one hand, this trait enables them to wander from place to place, and in some measure builds up a cosmopolitan perception in which countries, states, and certain ways of life are no more than external frameworks. But on the other hand, it leads to a degree of dissociation, in the sense that a person can go from one place to another without striking roots too deeply in any particular place.

We Are Quintessentially a Stiff-Necked People

Another trait that is found among Jews, which is actually essential to their existence, is a high degree of stubbornness. From this we may understand that every Jew who did not have the ability to cling—stubbornly, steadfastly, ceaselessly—to his identity, his faith, the structural pattern of his life, would not have had the ability to continue to exist, or at least to continue existing as a Jew. This stubbornness is part of the structural makeup, the essential nature, of the Jew. In principle, it is this obduracy—"for it is a stiff-necked people" (Exodus 32:9, 34:9; Deuteronomy 9:13, 10:16)—that is the basis for the hold on the very essence of being a Jew, of remaining a Jew, and, in another sense, of remaining alive at all. However, like all other character traits, it does not confine itself only to the sphere of beliefs and opinions, but pervades all other aspects of the mind and of life. So a person whose stubbornness and persistence are no longer directed at maintaining Judaism still retains these qualities but directs them to other aims—either to business and material success, or to intellectual enterprises and so on.

A related Jewish trait, which also derives from both external and internal factors of choice, is a high degree of individualism. Jewish individualism also stems from the inner culture, since despite all the religious duties that are national, public, and communal, the main spiritual and religious duties of a Jew are essentially linked to his individual nature. Although Jewish religious life is always centered on a core community, and it is very difficult to maintain a fully satisfying life without the necessary organized support of the community (the *minyan*), the actual existence of Jewish life does not depend on others. For example, a Jew does not need—or at least is not required—to conduct his prayers specifically in the synagogue, just as he does not need the services of a priest, since most of his duties are between him and God alone.

Moreover, life in the Diaspora, although founded on a well-developed system of mutual support, could not create clear and requisite frameworks within which a Jew could conduct his own way of life. With no army or work organizations that demanded cooperation, the "Jewish" professions—those in which Jews were able to engage and that were founded mainly on private initiative and not on the support from work within a firm—all produced a type of a person who was basically individualistic. The Jew was forced to be a person who constructs his way of life for himself and chooses his own profession, without needing help from the outside. He even chooses the kind of profession that he can take with him from place to place with relative ease.

⟶ We Are Buoyed by Faith ⟵

Yet another trait that derives from the essential Jewish nature is the ability to believe; another, even more so, is the deep need for faith. This is self-evident, because whoever does not have within himself the inner strength and deep longings for the life of faith is incapable of withstanding the external and internal pressure of being a Jew. It is not possible to follow God as a Jew should do—and with the whole system of internal difficulties that this entails and the enormous external pressures as well—except on the basis of a deep core of faith.

Whoever does not have faith—does not have the ability to construct his life on the basis of concerns other than real and immediate materialistic considerations—is incapable of continuing to live as a Jew. Such ability and compulsion to believe are, perhaps, what has most distinguished essential Jewishness since its formation.

The very first choice of Israel was the choice of belief and this choice strengthened increasingly over the generations, because it is impossible to be a Jew without it. Because of this, even when, for some reason, this or that individual Jew abandoned his faith, or was not raised in it, this did not change the essence of it, this basic spiritual quality. This Jew remains by force of nature an idealist, a person who by inner compulsion cannot live life simply but must live it for some idea. He must believe, because belief is an essential part of his psychological structuring, and he could not escape from it even if he wished to do so.

In addition to the general ability to believe, to be closely linked and subservient to some superior essence, some transcendental aim, the Jew has a special psychological structure that may be called the Messiah complex. (See Chapter 6, which explores the Jewish Messiah complex, in this book.) That is to say, the belief in the Messiah is not merely a passive faith in redemption, but is an inner urge to bring redemption nearer. This urge is not only an essential component of the Jewish religion, but also an element in the continued existence of the Jew *per se*.

The Jew does not merely feel committed and subservient to some higher purpose, but also feels a strong need to redeem reality, to reform it, to improve it. No one can continue a life of distress and insecurity, in which he is sometimes despised and humiliated by others, unless he feels a deep sense of mission. Here, too, the individual Jew may lose his messianic faith, but he is incapable of losing his need to hasten the redemption.

Whenever he hears, or thinks, that there are tidings of redemption, the Jew is always found among the first to try to realize it, whether it concerns the national redemption of states in which the Jews are always the foremost patriots, or with social redemption, or with any other attempt to change the structure of the world in order to improve it.

Another facet of the Jewish character, both essential and acquired, which is connected with this search for redemption, is that of intellectualism. This intellectualism emerges mainly from within, because unlike members of other religions, every Jew is bound by his religious faith to be learned in the Torah. Moreover, study in Jewish culture is not merely the study of the principles of faith, but is a complex matter of a highly intellectual character, as expressed in Talmudic literature, which comprises the major body of Jewish religious literature. In addition, social stratification that places the scholar at the top of the Jewish hierarchy, while those with other talents such as leadership or political standing are at a secondary level, creates conceptual and social pressure for intellectual achievement—an achievement that is mainly a religious one.

The typical age-old dream of the Jewish mother—that her son will be a rabbi—expresses a combination of the inward Jewish desire with the dream of social advancement. Whoever has been unread has found himself on the margins of society, and has always tried—if not for himself, at least for his children—to reach a higher standard, not only with the aim of social advancement, but also to consummate and fulfill his Jewishness more perfectly. For this reason, intellectual application was part of the Jewish character even when it was no longer directed toward the dream of the son's becoming a rabbi. Intellectual life was still seen as a goal to which one should aspire, and study of all kinds as a way of life that gives satisfaction in itself.

～ Our Qualities, Like All Qualities, ～ Are Double-Sided

These essential Jewish qualities, like all psychological qualities, are basically neutral. This means that like all other qualities of the mind, these can find various means of expression, both positive and negative, that are not necessarily contradictory, and their moral or social value fluctuates according to the conditions and ways in which they find expression.

The power of survival, for example, is a positive factor not only for the individual but also for the impetus that it gives to life and the attitude of respect that it expresses toward life and the continuity of existence. But this power can take on ugly forms of "pushiness," of an attempt to obtain something at any price, of sacrificing values in order to continue to survive or in order to conquer and acquire more things.

Flexibility, which is so vital for survival, can be of great value as the ability to learn and change, to grow and adapt oneself to reality. But on the other hand, it can also reach the point of total loss of self-respect, a complete lack of spine, uncontrolled pandering without any guidelines. The ability to imitate and simulate, which is on the one hand an instrument for learning and for emulation, on the other hand can descend to the level of mimicry, of aping, of a cheap representation created without any self-esteem.

The ability to move easily from place to place opens paths to the wider world, a world that is not limited, narrow, and coerced, yet at the same time it can create dissociation and a lack of attachment to any place, a lack of ability to take hold of anything, because nothing has stability or permanence.

The more internal qualities such as individualism can, on the one hand, provide an incentive to broaden the individual and raise him to a much higher level, to enable him to express himself and not to be assimilated by the herd, not to be effaced by general opinion but to make a stand on his own particular individuality. However, it might also prevent the possibility of teamwork, of cooperative ventures, and even descend to lower expressions of selfishness determined by ego alone.

Intellectualism, which is on the one hand an instrument for advancement, for enhancement, for broadening of the mind, can also be a way to stifle natural spontaneity and the ability to react emotionally as a human being to various situations. Even the ability to believe and the need for faith, which are such important elements in Jewish existence, can reach a stage of degeneration in the enthusiasm to create new cults, in becoming caught up by false opinions and inanities of every kind that the desire to believe creates in order to be attached to them, with a compulsion that has no inward control.

Also, the wish to save the world, to bring glad tidings, just as it is an instrument of enhancement, can also gradually regress into a wish to change and overturn things without building anything in their place, the need to "save" without taking into account the price or the need for all this.

Generally speaking, those very qualities that create the inward character of the Jew are not the choice of the individual. Each person receives these qualities as an inheritance from his ancestors, generation after generation, from all those fathers and mothers who have survived, and who have been selected as capable of carrying the burden of Judaism. However, what the individual receives is only the whole body of primary qualities, and he has the choice as to how they should be used. He has to define their value and essential nature, what they aim at and in what way they can reach perfection.

∽ Questions and Answers ∽

Q *How can we learn to use and not abuse our character traits?*

Rabbi Adin Steinsaltz (RS) We have certain character traits, as every private person has character traits. Nice people try to develop the good and desirable character traits. They try to suppress or at least to divert other traits, to use them only on special occasions.

If you are a hothead by nature, at some point you can learn to control yourself. That doesn't mean that you become a completely mild person, but rather you try to use your heat only at the times and places where it is needed.

Some people are sometimes too subtle for their own good. They have to know that the ability to make excuses is a good thing, but it shouldn't be used with friends, only with adversaries. That is what people do. If I have a map of my own character, I find some things desirable and some undesirable, so I try to deal with them. I deal with them in the same way as you arrange a household. You have so much furniture, and you cannot get rid of most of it, so you put the fancy chair in one room and the old broken chair in another. One chair should be used for firewood, and one should be used when company visits.

Q *You say that there are positive and negative aspects of character traits and that one of the character traits of the Jewish people is flexibility. Could you offer an example of a positive and a negative manifestation of this trait?*

RS Flexibility is very useful for many things in life, for the ability to change one's profession or to change one's affiliation when it is needed. Flexibility can also become a complete lack of any backbone, and that becomes dangerous.

Q *What about persistence?*

RS Persistence and obstinacy are enormously important and Jews have been known, and are alternately proud and not proud, for being hard-headed and unable to move. Determining which things are important and which are not is the essence of life. They may be your family, your environment, your chosen way of life. The ability to be persistent and to go on and not allow yourself to be diverted is important here. On the other hand, if a person becomes obstinate about any kind of little thing, then it is basically damaging. So I have to decide that I will be obstinate only about important things.

Q *What about the will to live? Is there a negative side to the will to live?*

RS It has to be remembered that there are times when a person has to make a choice for death. There are borders that go even beyond death, and if a person does not have these borders he becomes a despicable kind of creature.

Chapter V

Is Money Our God?

The Slander, Lies, and Misunderstandings Regarding Jews and Money

The close relationship between Jews and money is infamous throughout the world. Jews are regarded as money dealers, as expert and successful in financial transactions, and also as the possessors of enormous sums of money. The very word *Jew*, both as noun and verb, has been connected in various languages with money dealing. This use of the word *Jew* exists in a few European languages, generally in a negative sense, and it is still found in dictionaries and manuals, in spite of the efforts of various Jewish groups to eliminate this meaning of the word, at least from standard dictionaries.

All this connection of Jews with money was done by a kind of general consensus. In certain places it was accepted as a neutral fact, whereas in many others it was taken in a negative and hostile sense because Jews were perceived as those who were intensely absorbed in matters concerning money and money alone. Marx, for example, expressed this view by saying that the secular god of the Jews was money.

These views were accepted as the simple truth by many nations, including those in which the number of Jews was very small, and even among those that had no Jews at all. Moreover, such assumptions were made not only by non-Jews—out of hatred or jealousy—but also to some extent from an internal viewpoint. Although the subject has not been extensively discussed in Jewish sources, we do find it mentioned in sermons and ethical works, and more so in Jewish folklore, stories, and popular jokes. In all these, the assumption that Jews frequently deal in money matters, and that they are obsessed with and deeply involved in the pursuit of money, is accepted quite simply. But in reality, this was never exactly so.

~ The Myth of Jewish Wealth ~

Most of the Jews in history were not money dealers, and in those places where there were a large number of Jewish traders and peddlers, the majority of them dealt in various crafts, whether in religious artifacts or other types of creative craftsmanship. In addition, the assumption that Jews, if only a minority of them, held the highest percentage of all the money in the world is not true and never was true. Even in periods when some Jews were tremendously rich, like the House of Rothschild in France, and in some places where they were bank owners, Jews have not possessed the largest fortunes and never attained much wealth.

From the perspective of Jewish history, the idea that Jews and money were considered nearly identical concepts is relatively new. Until the beginning of the Middle Ages, and in some places even for centuries afterwards, most Jews were farmers; the number of merchants was very limited and the number of money dealers even more so. The Jewish people were mainly agricultural workers, and a large percentage of them were craftsmen in practical vocations. Tradesmen, especially those who were exclusively in business, were very few in number.

Furthermore, the very existence of Jewish traders was a novel phenomenon. In the Biblical period, for example, Jews seem to have been mainly tillers of the soil, and were not engaged in commerce at all. Some Jews at the end of the Biblical period were mercenary soldiers, a profession for which we find evidence in the early centuries of the Second Temple period.

The basic economic structure at the time consisted of landowning families whose land, according to the laws of the Torah, was under tenure and was never to be transferred. Side by side with them were the artisans whose work was done in addition to their landowning activities. One of the most prominent proofs of this is that the term used for a trader was *Canaanite*—meaning that the Jew was not a trader, and those who engaged in trade among the Jews were strangers, Canaanites. Even the Torah commandments that strongly and unequivocally prohibited Jews from taking interest from other Jews made it very difficult to create any viable money market as long as most of them were closely attached to their land.

The transition into the financial market began with their exile, when the Jews were uprooted from their country and their lands. Yet even this change was only to a partial degree. Large urban centers such as Alexandria certainly had a significant number of Jewish merchants, but it appears that most Jews were—and continued to be for centuries in most countries—artisans, and some of them soldiers.

Most of the very large and well-established community of Jews in Babylon remained an agricultural community, and the farmers supplemented their income by engaging in minor crafts and to a limited extent in peddling. Very few Jews engaged in extensive trading or were exclusively involved in the commercial professions.

We Had Been Forbidden to Own Land

The uprooting of the Jews from agricultural work was accomplished much later, with the rise and dominance of Christianity and, to a great extent, also that of Islam. The social structure, which gradually became more and more feudal in nature, could not include the Jewish landowners as an integral part of it, because land ownership—especially the ownership of large tracts of land— was the prerogative of people at a certain social level that was associated with some central ruling power on one hand and with church rule on the other.

For generations, an ever-increasing number of laws were passed against the Jews, until in most European countries it was prohibited for Jews to own any land at all. Moreover, the urban centers, which began to receive independent status, and were partially organized by merchant guilds and by large craftsmen's guilds, resolutely prevented the entry of Jews into their ranks.

At the end of the Middle Ages, new laws denied Jews entry into nearly all the free professions, and for this reason they were driven by necessity into whatever positions were still left open to them. These occupations were to a large extent found in the financial market and in money lending with usury, as well as minor trading and craftsmanship that were not included in the official craftsmen's guilds.

In addition to these externally applied laws, there was also the internal feeling of uncertainty within the stable existence of every Jewish community. During the Middle Ages, the expulsion of Jews occurred more and more frequently, and it was understood that whoever had no right to established residence, and no confidence regarding his continued habitation in any place, could not invest in real estate that could not be quickly transferred to others. Thus, even if Jews had had the legal ability to obtain ownership of a piece of land, it would have had very little chance of being permanent in view of the general social and political structure.

Of course, throughout the world, including Europe, more especially in Eastern countries, there were still some Jewish farmers. But they became a negligible minority; the ordinary Jew had to gain his livelihood through trade or through the existing financial markets.

During the many generations in which Jews have lived in exile, most Jews have been poor, and at times even destitute. By force of circumstance, the Jews were usually poorer than the general population. For this reason, it is surprising that the widespread impression was created about Jewish wealth and Jewish money.

Of course, in every generation there were rich Jews, and even very rich Jews, and their alien status must have given greater prominence to their special position of wealth. To this was added a certain tendency toward ostentation that existed among a number of rich Jews who displayed their wealth in ways that caused much envy. From the Middle Ages onward there were a number of community rulings, court bans, and warnings by rabbis against behaving in an ostentatious manner for fear that it would lead to anti-Semitic outbursts. These repeated warnings indicate that there were substantial reasons for them to be made. But the existence of a number of rich Jews does not necessarily create a general picture or impression to such an intense degree.

~ Myth of Jewish Wealth Persists ~

The real reason for this impression of Jews and the large amount of money they held was quite different. Its origins were in the general error of perception that nearly everyone, from the Middle Ages onward, had fallen into. At nearly every level of medieval society, land and its crops were the main source of wealth, and wealth was derived only to a far lesser degree from finished or partially finished products. Money was merely the surplus that could be created from exceptionally successful crops, or from the need to exchange commodities not by barter but by purchase. For this reason, the amount of money that was visible was relatively small. On the other hand, money for Jews did not come from production surpluses, but was the basic source of their assets.

Even though this seems to be understood, it was not clearly evident. The farmer hardly ever used money; if he ever did have any use for it at all, it was only for very small sums, and when he managed to accumulate a small sum of money he was then a rich man. That same farmer could see much greater sums of money in the hands of a Jew, and it would be difficult for him to grasp that that money was equal to only a small portion of the property in land, animals, and products he himself possessed. The error was therefore very simple: since the Jew had so much more money, it meant that he was much richer.

That same error could also be found among people at a higher social level. Even the nobles of the Middle Ages and the period that followed mainly possessed land and all that this entailed. Ready money that was apparent to the eye was therefore only a small part of their wealth. And undoubtedly, whenever they had need for a much larger amount of money, they found it difficult to obtain.

On the other hand, the merchant, and specifically the Jewish financier, possessed large sums of money and could easily lend it or trade with it. It is therefore understandable that not only farmers, but also the higher nobility and the kings, imagined the almost inexhaustible Jewish wealth. It was in this error of perception that the belief in Jewish greed was rooted.

We Have Lived a Subsistence Existence

As mentioned earlier, although there is not much statistical evidence for very distant historical periods, it is clear that most Jews were always extremely poor. Jews were always being pushed aside economically into the margins of society, and could not participate in those professions that yielded larger incomes. Whether this was brought about by well-defined laws or by pressure from the urban residents or merchant guilds, there was an enormous pressure against their participation in anything profitable, even in those professions they were theoretically permitted to engage in, such as trade.

Lending with interest was one of the few things Jews could do. It always entailed risk, whether the risk was that the loan would not be paid because the borrower could not meet the debt, or that the lender would not be able to demand the payment forcefully enough.

In many ways the situation of the impoverished Jews—and, as mentioned earlier, this meant most of the Jews—was worse than that of the farmers. In the course of years (excluding, of course, the times of special troubles, drought, floods, or wars, which naturally affected everyone, especially the Jews), even the poorest farmer could be sure that he would have at least the minimal amount of food to satisfy his hunger. Even when he did not have money for luxuries, working on the land, in addition to a small number of household goods, could supply his basic needs. This was not so for the Jew, who had no land of his own and could certainly die of starvation simply for the lack of means to provide for his immediate minimal needs.

In most of the colder European countries, bread to eat and wood to burn in the oven were a matter of life and death for most Jews, both in the villages and in the larger towns. The Jewish trader of Eastern Europe was no more than a mere peddler, who conducted his bartering on the most basic level and depended for his existence on the small profit that the population around him, which was generally made up of poor people as well, could afford to give him. For strangers who observed this from afar, Jewish economic activity might seem to be an avaricious attack motivated by a greed for profit. But the eagerness and desire to obtain some profit (and whatever accompanied it, good or bad), the attempt to gain as much profit as possible in any deal, and sometimes even to cheat the other side—all this was caused not by avarice but by starvation, in the most basic sense of the word.

The Jewish peddler who waited longingly for market days, the small-town merchant who spent a whole day going around the markets, did not only deal in money, but also thought about money, and to a certain degree was immersed in money matters—not because money was an object of greedy desire, and not even because of a desire for power or money in itself, but because this was the only way he could obtain the means for minimal existence.

Jewish moral thinkers, however much they rebuked the members of their community for being so immersed in matters of trade, accounts, and financial stratagems, knew that all this was the only way open to most of the Jews to exist at all.

An expression of distress in this desperate attempt to live is the prayer for subsistence that is found in many prayer books, as well as the supplications and entreaties on the same subject. One of the Hasidic leaders who was famous for his penetrating observations, spoken in a jesting tone, used to say, "If we put all the Jewish prayers into the barrel of a cannon and fired it, a single penny would emerge." But he himself added, "If we take this same penny and put it into the cannon and fire it, only Torah and good deeds would emerge from it: money to pay the *melamed* (religious teacher) for the children; a little needed for charity; and whatever is necessary for self-existence."

∼ Community Self-Sufficiency ∼ Made Jewish Poverty Less Obvious

Jewish poverty was not visible to outsiders. The Jewish beggars, widows, and orphans, that is, all those who could not gain their own livelihood and were in need of assistance, were rarely seen in non-Jewish society. The Jewish community could hardly ever depend on any kind of help from the authorities or from private persons to support its poor. All these, including the many people who were engaged in Torah study, either teaching it or learning it (for example, rabbis, judges, and cantors), needed to be supported by the meager resources of the Jewish community in order to maintain a certain level of scholarship that was vital for the continuation of Jewish existence. Yet strangers on the outside who came into frequent contact with Jews saw only two aspects of Jewish life: the presumed wealth of the Jews in ready money, and their pursuit of any kind of profit.

Of course, the constant dealing in money and trade, and the need for some kind of profit, must have a certain degree of influence on the inward soul of a person, and his world view is shaped by what he needs to do, whether for his own good or not, in the course of his life. All that a person does during his lifetime, even if he does not do it out of some special desire, has an influence on his way of thinking. When a farmer looks up at the sky, it is usually not in order to see the beauty of the stars but to know if there are any rain clouds.

Similarly, money dealing, a necessity that the Jew could not avoid, caused many Jews not only to deal in trade and finance but also to think and dream about them. It sometimes happens that the evil desire for certain things remains even when the necessity that caused it no longer exists. In this sense, the evil desire for money is no different from other such inclinations. To a large extent it is the product not only of an inner urge but also of habit, a habit that can become second nature, and the pursuit of money can become so habitual that people pursue it even when they do not need it.

∽ Economics Is Not ∾ Central to Jewish Life

Despite all this, even after many generations of dealing in money and financial matters, Jewish society has never reached a stage at which the pursuit of money or its acquisition was an end in itself.

One of the foremost reasons that the Jewish people did not become one that aspired to wealth lies in the very essence of Judaism and in the spiritual and social structures it created. These structures, which have endured throughout the generations of Jewish existence, have had a decisive impact on Jews' ways of thinking, and have prevented the economic factor from being the central one in their life experience.

Generally speaking, it may be said that to a great extent Judaism relates to poverty and riches indifferently. There are, of course, a few sayings in praise of poverty, but ultimately, poverty was never considered a virtue or a good in itself. Neither was it considered a reason for shame, nor an expression of sin, but mainly it was thought of as one of the many situations in which a person could be found. Moreover, there are some essential laws in Judaism that stress the idea of not wasting money so as not to become impoverished.

Just as there are many tales about great sages and famous people who were poor, and who in spite of their poverty—sometimes because of their poverty—reached spiritual and intellectual heights, there are also stories about other people who were no less able to attain such heights and were also rich men. Sages have discussed these problems extensively, and essentially have spoken about the need to resist the temptations of wealth and also the need to resist the temptations and snares of poverty.

The essence of this view can be found in the Book of Proverbs: ". . . give me neither poverty nor riches; provide me with my daily bread" (Proverbs 30:8). Such words embody the general Jewish attitude toward this world: even if life in this world and everything it contains are not considered to be the purpose of a man's life, there is still no reason to renounce or destroy them in order to attain some higher aim. We are to use whatever exists in the world, both its merits and its negative qualities, so as to advance to a higher level.

But there are other aspects of the Jewish world that have prevented the economic factor—and thus the pursuit of a higher economic status—from becoming the basic, essential force in life. True, in every generation rich people have had power and influence far beyond their numerical strength in the community or the nation as a whole. Yet the real aristocracy of the Jewish people was that of Torah study. At the highest level of Jewish society was not the rich man but the wise man. Standing at the head of a community, engaging in the leadership of the people, were the Torah sages. Money in itself was a source of power, but usually the ruling authority of the community sages had higher importance and validity.

Thus, a person who was merely rich was not esteemed because of his status, but only if he succeeded in connecting himself with the basic aristocracy: the aristocracy of the learned scholars. The social phenomenon of the rich man who marries his daughter to a Torah scholar, even if the scholar is poor, was well known and widely practiced, and it derived from the fact that authority and status lay in wisdom and not in money. The dream of the Jewish mother that her son would be a rabbi was an attainable dream, both because the aristocracy of learning, unlike that of money, was much more accessible to whoever had the will and talent, and because it was supported by the general religious perception. This perception, that the wise man was an authority, was not only because of his wisdom but also because he was on a superior level by virtue of his holier status.

⌒ Wisdom Above Riches ⌒

Thus, although the rich had much greater power and enormous economic influence, they were subject to the authority of the sages. Because of the vicissitudes of time, few rich families could keep their wealth for generations, yet there were many multi-generational dynasties of Talmudic sages. Quite often, the descendants of rich families turned away from the world of business to the world of Torah learning. Also, the general Jewish view of money was essentially as an instrument rather than as an end, mainly serving to further what was considered to be the fundamental purpose of life: the fulfillment of the Torah commandments.

It should be remembered that for many generations Jewish communities had no means of real enforcement of accepted communal behavior. Even the most serious means of coercion that they possessed—expulsion from the community by a ban (which was actually used very sparingly)—did not have any validity without the consent and implicit attitude of those concerned. Funds needed by the community as a whole, or by individuals within it, had to come from within. For this reason, the person who had money was accustomed and even conditioned not to use it only for himself but to use it also for the needs of others, either by charitable donations or by supporting Torah study in every possible way.

It was also often impossible for the rich to spend their wealth on those things that the gentile rich could acquire. Many luxuries were barred to Jews, either because of state laws or because of the principles of Jewish law. The rich Jew could not, therefore, build himself palaces and magnificent gardens, nor could he spend his money on horses and mistresses. For that reason, if he wanted to make any use of his money he had to transfer it to causes that were considered more important and more respectable in the community: to charitable enterprises such as building synagogues or Torah academies, support for the poor, and similar causes.

All these factors had a powerful influence. To a certain degree, they became part of the collective consciousness and continued to have an effect even on those people who were not connected to the same extent—or even connected at all—to the Jewish religion. Marx's famous saying, that the secular religion of the Jews was money, is therefore not merely a personal reflection from the outside, but also an expression of a Jewry that had broken out of the confines of its framework. The stereotypes persist even long after they have lost any justification, and therefore there is not much chance that the perception of Jews from the outside will change very quickly. Yet from the Jew's perspective about his own society, he still remains in the same situation and adheres to the same position he held in former generations, namely that money is merely a secondary factor in the totality of his continued existence. There are other dreams and other aspirations that fill his heart.

⟋ Questions and Answers ⟍

Q *Do you think it's even practical to try to change the stereotypes regarding Jews and money?*

Rabbi Adin Steinsaltz (RS) In some places, it would surely be helpful. But when trying to change something that is embedded in the minds of people, you must realize that you are working against inertia. Inertia is not something that you can easily overcome. Even one person is very hard to change.

Sometimes, even after you prove something, a person will say, "Well, it was very well done, very well said, but still Jews have more money." Sometimes there will be a proof but it won't do any good. You can find huge numbers of Jewish beggars, people who are poor to the point of starvation. It hasn't changed the notion that all Jews are rich.

Q *When I asked my daughter's friend, whose Jewish family comes from Iran, if she knew what her family did for a living, she said she thought that one of her grandfathers had been a money lender. One of us sitting there said, "Oh, they must have been rich!" You make the* *point, though, that being a money lender didn't mean you were rich at all.*

RS Not at all! You think this because you are not a money lender. If you were a money lender, you would know that it means you get 3 percent profit and are poorer than many of the other people around you.

Q *How do we avoid turning money into an end rather than a means?*

RS Money, by its very definition, is never an end. It is a way of exchanging, of acquiring things. When it becomes an obsession, when it becomes an end in itself, that obsession is a slightly pathological situation. This is true about anything. Chewing is a way of eating. When a person begins to chew before he eats, it is a sign of an illness. Washing your hands is very important to cleanliness. When you see a person washing his hands sixty times a day, it is a sign of compulsiveness. Money is a way of transforming assets into other things, whatever they are. If it becomes a purpose in itself, that is defined psychologically as a perversion. This is exactly the definition of a perversion: in perversion, you have something that is auxiliary but that becomes a purpose in itself.

Chapter VI

Why Do We Want to Save the World?

Exploring the Jewish Messiah Complex

J ust as there are individual psychological complexes, so there are psychological complexes in an entire nation. To the extent that we can speak about the aims, ambitions, and dreams of a people, it is also possible to speak about the complexes that belong to and affect this people. One such complex is the Jewish Messiah complex.

Certainly there are people who suffer from a persecution complex, or a superiority or inferiority complex. Sometimes it is possible to give a sufficient historical answer to the question of why a certain complex or psychosis develops within a certain people, and sometimes there is no clear and rational explanation for it. In any case, such complexes, like other national definitions, belong to and affect the whole. It may be said that when the larger part of a certain nation acts with a measure of unity and solidarity, it reveals character traits or behavior patterns that can be attributed to the entire nation.

As with any large generalization, one may find many particular individuals who do not fit into the generality. Moreover, at times a certain character trait or quality belongs only to the general public, while the individuals themselves do not possess these qualities more recognizably than do other nations and peoples. It is only when a large group of people acts in unison that a certain quality can be recognized in it, whether positive or negative, even though that quality does not appear in the individuals within that group, or that is found in them only to a minor extent.

The difference between the behavior of particular individuals and communal groups is a well-known phenomenon, and there is no doubt that individuals act, and to some extent even sense and feel, differently from the general masses. Mass psychology is different from the way in which each of the individuals who make up a group will act for himself. However, there are also national complexes that are not necessarily part of the general public experience, but affect the soul of each individual. In such cases, the general public acts as a combination of individuals, each of whom possesses that psychological quality.

⟶ The Jewish Mission ⟵

The Jewish people, not only in its overall national experience, but also in the particular individual experiences of each person, suffer from a Messiah complex. A complex is a phenomenon, or psychological desire, that is found in the human heart. It does not appear in any conscious form within the person, but the complex nevertheless acts on him, and he does things caused by its motivating force without being aware of their true inner reasons.

The Messiah complex is the desire, the ambition, the urge to be the Messiah, to be the redeemer and savior of the world. It is not only a general desire, obscure or overt, to save the world or to improve its condition. It has another component, no less important, which is the ambition of the personal ego to *be* the redeemer of the world.

The sages have said of the verse "Do not touch my anointed one" (Psalm 105:15) that "these are the infants of the rabbinical schools." The little children, the pupils in the schools, all wish to be the Messiah—a Jewish child grows, or perhaps is even born, with the desire to be the Messiah. For this reason, all schoolchildren are "messianic-minded": each of them is like a little Messiah; and even if he is not the Messiah, either because of his present level of ability or his future potential, he nevertheless is a part of the Messiah by virtue of his desire and his dream.

∽ A Spark of the Messiah ∼

Thus, according to the Jewish inner world view, it may be said that every Jew harbors in some way a spark of the Messiah. In this sense, just as we believe that every Jew bears a spark of the patriarchs and shepherds of the nation—Abraham, Isaac, and Jacob—which he inherits as part of his essential legacy, so does every Jew bear a spark of the Messiah that he is about to realize, that in this sense is a spark of the future. The Messiah to be revealed is the collection of all these sparks throughout all the generations into one personality, the final sum of a certain quality that is found in all Jews, and that reaches its perfect expression in one man who includes them all within himself.

The essence of the messianic idea, in its original meaning, is the redemption of Israel, the wish to restore the Jewish people to its former glory, to renew the glorious Jewish kingdom in the fullest sense. But the messianic idea is also a much wider thing, because the redemption of Israel is only a stage, a certain step, in the comprehensive process of the redemption of the world as a whole.

Even in Judaism, however, there are disputed views with regard to the Messiah. There are those who see the Messiah as the entry into a new world reality, while others see in him an interim and very earthly stage on the way to a drastic difference in both the spiritual and the material world. Whatever the truth may be, everyone agrees on the unified perception of the Messiah as the redeemer of the world, one who will change reality. *Messiah* does not merely mean a new political structure, but also a new order in the essential relationship between people and between man and God, and, beyond this, in the structure and essential nature of the world in which we live. The Messiah is the key to this new world, a world in which there is no war, deprivation, or suffering, neither the sufferings of the soul nor the sufferings of the body.

The belief in the coming of the Messiah is not just a vague idea about a happier kind of reality. Unlike the belief in the survival of the soul and the good portion in the world to come, the belief in the Messiah is essentially a belief in the possibility of change in the reality of this world. In this belief there is also a protest against the difficulties, evils, sorrows, and sufferings of this world—the sorrows of the Jew as well as the sorrows of the world in general.

⟶ This World Must Be Changed ⟵

The Jewish belief in the advent of the Messiah is in itself a part of the perception of the mission of the Jewish people. But it is specifically in the messianic perception, with all its uniqueness, that there is an emphasis on the general commitment to reality as a whole, which is connected with the perception of the mission of Judaism as the means of changing and reforming the entire world. Moreover, whether or not a Jew thinks and acts in order to hasten the time of redemption, he still believes what he does is essential to the Messiah's coming. The messianic aim is therefore not the hope, but the desire—followed by actual activity of whatever form—that the Messiah come into the world.

The significance of the messianic belief is the shift of focus of religious commitment and Jewish affiliation from being entirely something rooted in the past to a goal for the future. Judaism is therefore not just a movement that perpetuates past glories, nor is it only the collective power to keep that earlier momentum going. Because of the messianic drive, Judaism is also an aspiration toward a future of redemption.

Bringing redemption nearer is not only a national duty or a general belief. It takes place within the scope of the commandments (the *mitzvot*) and it becomes a matter for the individual, whose good deeds—in general or in particular—bring redemption nearer. In the same way, perversions and sins delay redemption and prevent the coming of the Messiah.

The messianic "idea" is not simply an idea, but much more than that. It is a motivating, stimulating force, and it serves as a means to create things or to persist in doing them. Yes, it has an intellectual form as an idea and as a theological notion. But when it is internalized, it also has an effect on the mind. The messianic mission is not just a reference point in the perception of the future. It also turns into a messianic dream. That is to say, as a dream of life it is part of the internal structure of life. It is something that acts not only on the intellectual part of the mind and spirit but also on their depths and secret mysteries.

⟳ The Dream Lives Large ⟳ in Our Children

The messianic dream finds its most perfect and revealed expression in children. Why is this? It is simply because they are children. Because they are younger, they are more sensitive to meanings: these are not specifically matters that have any formal definitions. Children sometimes cannot understand or do not wish to understand definitions, but they have a feeling for dreams. Just as children say, openly and forthrightly, those things that adults whisper secretly, they also dream openly what adults do not always express in an explicit and open manner. Because they are young, they accept ideas with greater enthusiasm, and also with greater simplicity, and they cling to them—even if in a childish manner—with all their hearts.

Moreover, children have a quality of innocence, of naïveté. Adults—because they have more experience and wider understanding—know, or understand in a certain manner, the difficul-

ties that stand in the way of carrying out a task. They also understand its enormous scope, and in accordance with this understanding they can estimate how difficult it is to complete.
Children, on the other hand—precisely because of their lack of
real knowledge and their inexperience, and their inability to comprehend all the aspects of the matter—take things with extreme
simplicity.

In other words, the adult can measure his limitations and
assess what he is capable of, and, even more so, what he is totally
incapable of doing. However, such barriers do not exist for the
child, and certainly cannot stand in the way of his dreams. Since
he has no idea of his human and personal limitations, there is
nothing to prevent him from planning, dreaming, and wanting
things that perhaps can never be actually realized. Therefore, the
Jewish child dreams the messianic dream—not only in its shape as
a grand objective, as a general dream, but as a private dream, as a
personal wish for me myself to be the one who will create this new
reality—and for this reason the children of the rabbinical schools
are messianic.

What happens to the children when they become adults?
Through the continuous learning of the facts of life, of all kinds,
they lose the innocence of childhood. They learn that every
change—not only in the whole world, but even in a small part of
it—is an enormous task, almost impossible. They learn to realize
their own limitations. A child can believe that he is capable of
doing everything; as he grows up, he begins to realize the limitations of his power, both because he is a single individual and
because of the limitations of his talents and abilities.

Furthermore, the life of an adult forces him to create an
order of priorities. By force of nature and because of the pressures
of life, people generally choose to do those things that a person
must do within a short time, or, at least, those things that they
think they are actually capable of doing. People are immersed in

work, family life, and various other occupations, and have no time for dreams, and the dreams turn into a marginal element in their experience.

⁓ From Dream to Complex ⁓

What happens then to the dream about the Messiah? This dream is not altogether effaced; it is not discarded like an unwanted object. But it is transferred to less emotional spheres—less demanding of general faith—of activity in many fields of endeavor that do not require immersion in this dream. And since the messianic dream is not merely a wish that good things will come, a hope for a wonderful future that will occur some time, but has a high degree of exigency, it is pushed away like other childish dreams and disappears from everyday thinking, and sometimes even from conscious thought.

However, these rejected dreams are also not effaced: they enter in various ways into the depths of experience. What was once an openly avowed dream, an explicit wish, now becomes something hidden within the secret places of the soul, a hidden power that interferes with and is entangled in the business of life; that is to say, it becomes a complex. Since the messianic aim is such an essential component of the overall national desire, it has become part of personal consciousness. And so, if it does not find expression in open and explicit thought, it finds expression as a secret and hidden desire.

Many children, and even to some extent many adults, dream of greatness. Many children dream, at one stage or another of their lives, of being monarchs, rulers, soldiers, conquerors of the world and its sovereigns. The messianic dream has some similarity to such dreams, which are part of that childish ability to think and imagine great and wonderful deeds without taking into account how they may be carried out practically. But the messianic dream is not merely a dream of greatness: in a certain sense, within the dream itself lies the uniqueness of the messianic experience. The desire for personal greatness is merely a part of the messianic dream, which is essentially the bringing of redemption to others. The main problem of the Messiah is not his greatness—either his greatness or the greatness of his rule—but the situation of the other, of others, of the world.

In order to want to be the Messiah, a person has to know and to sense—either openly or in a very obscure manner—the destitution of his people, the suffering and want of the nation, and to a larger extent the problems and pains of the world. The messianic sense emerges from the feeling that reality needs to be altered, that the condition of the world imposes a heavy task on a person: to bring it to a state of change, reform, and redemption.

For this reason, at the center of the messianic dreams, in all its manifestations, stands the other person, not the self. The problem, the suffering and want of the other arouses this sense within the self. That is to say, since others are in distress, I am the one who wishes, who longs, and who sometimes is even committed, obliged, and forced to *be* the deliverer and savior.

∽ An Unconscious Burden ∽

The messianic dream exists but is repressed even among the faithful believers. Among those who say every day that they believe with perfect faith in the coming of the Messiah, the personal dream has become a repressed one, because even if a person still believes with all his heart that redemption will come, and lives in expectation of it every day, he no longer dreams that he himself will be the savior and redeemer, nor does he long for that role.

However, this repression is even greater among those Jews who no longer openly believe in the messianic aim. A significant number, perhaps the majority, of Jewish children today—and even more so the adults—grow up as people for whom Judaism is a burden of the past, and often a burden that they wish to shed. A Jew may be in his view partly a Jew, an agnostic, even an atheist, so what does belief in the Messiah mean to him?

In fact, as we have said, messianism is not only something that one is conscious of: messianism is part of the essence of the Jewish person *per se,* whether he desires it openly or does not desire it at all, whether he is conscious of it or is totally unaware of it. This is part of his collective unconscious, and it acts on him not only as a general national demand but as a personal conditioning of his own life, which influences his dreams and wishes. Even if the parents of a Jew have raised him to be totally deprived of any Jewish ideology, they cannot deprive him of his basic spiritual essence, the messianic dream—or at least the messianic complex.

Indeed, the messianic complex appears in Jews even when they no longer act as Jews in any explicit manner. This complex, even in its non-Jewish and nonreligious manifestations, includes within it a deep sensitivity to the suffering and distress in the world in general, to the suffering and distress of others. Moreover, beyond this sensitivity there is an additional element, which is also highly characteristic of the messianic sense. The sensitivity to the problems of the other is accompanied by a sense of duty to do something to improve the situation, or, on a larger scale, to save the world.

There are countless examples in which Jews, in any place whatsoever, have initiated, participated in, and been the leaders not only of campaigns, but of entire movements of freedom, of liberation from suffering—in other words, movements that attempt to reach some degree of redemption. The huge percentage of Jews participating in revolutionary movements is a phenomenon that does not need much proof. In fact, over the past few centuries, there has hardly been a revolutionary movement in which Jews did not take an active part. Even in places where the proportion of Jews in the population was small, the part they played in revolutionary movements was immeasurably great.

⟶ Fixing the World ⟵

If we examine it, we shall see that the focal point of all these movements is the desire to better the existing situation and to improve reality, whether it applies to national liberation or social liberation, whether these are movements that work in an extreme and revolutionary manner or whether they try to gain their objectives through teaching, influence, help, or support. They may be peace movements or movements for the liberation of the spirit; movements to improve the condition of starving, sick, and suffering people; or, beyond these, movements to improve the environment, to reform the world, to redeem reality in general.

As we have pointed out, one may indeed find an impressive percentage of Jews—including initiators and leaders—in movements of all kinds that apparently have nothing in common. Jews have participated with enthusiasm and great devotion in leftist movements, but also in revolutionary movements that were explicitly rightist. Jews have participated in and been active in movements that were essentially cosmopolitan, but, no less so, in liberation movements that were national and partisan. Jews have been active in many movements that were materialistic and atheistic by definition, but no less so in movements that had a deeply religious trend, not specifically Jewish.

What these movements have in common is not their particular ideology, but the general dream of redemption, that same dream that springs from seeing distress and understanding the need, from the denial of servitude and the wish to bring some part of the world—a state or a nation or a certain race—to a higher level. In other words, the dream contains the intention and the desire to bring redemption to the world.

Whenever Jews joined in liberation and redemption, either as leaders and initiators or as members and partners, they never asked how I (as a person, and sometimes as a nation) can benefit. The reason for this, as we have said, is that the Messiah complex is not based on the personal wish to attain greatness or influence, but on seeing what needs to be reformed, on the sense of duty to act in order to assist in this reform. This is the basic and primary urge; even if later on all kinds of wishes or desires are linked up with it, the point of departure is the need to help, to support, to assist in order to bring redemption to the world.

⟞ Our Underlying Dream ⟝

The rational question—"Who appointed you? Who gave you the authority to act in this sphere?"—is one that a Jew does not ask himself. But this question is often asked by those who feel threatened by such intervention, and quite often by those very people for whose sake the Jews are acting. Of course, in many instances—not only those in which Jews were the initiators and leaders—people have willingly accepted this help. But in many cases this gratitude was joined, almost from the start, by a sense of resentment: "What business is it of yours?" And sometimes this feeling is even accompanied by suspicion that someone is trying to take advantage of the movement or action for his own benefit. In any case, there is a lack of basic understanding as to what motivates these Jews to devote themselves, even to the extent of self-sacrifice, for the sake of others.

In every generation there have been Jews who have acted because they were Jews, that is to say, from a realization that their Jewishness obliged them to act for the sake of redeeming the world. But others continued to do so even when their ideological commitment to Judaism no longer existed, and even when they acted without any conscious reason, through an urge that they themselves were unable to explain. The Jewish urge to do such things does not come from what Jews are required to do, and certainly not because they have any conscious interest in doing so. This urge comes from an inner need that is aroused by suffering, especially the suffering of others.

Moses, who was the first savior of the Jewish people, began his work through that same urgency: to help those who were suffering, to right a wrong deed. He did so not because it was demanded of him, but because he was inwardly bound to do so, and he continued to do so even when those he tried to help were ungrateful, and even when they acted against him. The reason was that his drive was not derived from the wishes of others, but from something within him, from his own messianism.

All these urges are expressed not only in extreme revolutionary movements or in public activity, but also in small, personal, unimpressive actions. The same urge that induces a person to participate in a revolutionary movement may bring another person—of a different character, or with other challenges—to be a doctor or a social worker. However, in a basic sense, they are both motivated by the same force. At first it is not easy to see this, but the young revolutionary who tries to build a national atheistic liberation movement in a certain country, the pot-bellied doctor who treats sick people in a small town, or the tired teacher who sits and teaches the children of other people—all contain within themselves, unconsciously, the underlying dream of the Jewish child: to be the Messiah.

⤳ Questions and Answers ⤳

Q *Do groups other than Jews have a Messiah complex?*

Rabbi Adin Steinsaltz (RS) I would say that other people have it partially. In many cultures, there is something similar. It has happened in different ways within different cultures. There was once the notion, for example, of the white man's burden. That wasn't very far from it. There was also a very strong Messiah notion in Russia, not connected at all with Communism, but rather pre-Communist and national. This kind of notion some-times also had a beautiful literary expression. So I would say it's not unique.

Q *Do we raise our children with the Messiah complex in mind?*

RS As long as we raise them as Jews, and I'm speaking in the broadest sense of the word, we are raising them to do something special. Even when you don't say it in these words, it is always there. In smaller children, it can express itself better, but sometimes it erupts in adults also. When you raise a boy or a girl and you tell them, "You are Jewish," it has to have some meaning. What is the meaning of it? The meaning is this kind of specialness that is not a deformity but some kind of an additional package.

Q *Can you give a concise reason why Jews don't believe that Jesus was the Messiah?*

RS Being the Messiah is not a pure theological concept. The Messiah is the Redeemer, the person who makes life in this world different. That's what was said in the Middle Ages by the Nachmanides when he had the opportunity to speak up. You can't say that there's any redemption. You may say that in the

World to Come you will be redeemed, but that is not our notion of a Messiah. The reality is what is done here in the world. The wolf and the lamb are still in the same positions as they were two thousand years ago. The world of peace, plenty, and love has not come.

Chapter VII

Are We Excessively Warm or Excessively Cold?

The Seemingly Contradictory
Phenomena of Jewish Emotionalism
and Intellectualism

Jews have very often been defined, and also blamed, according to contradictory definitions and accusations. Years ago, it was acceptable in many cultures, from Nazi Germany to many Western European countries, and even in America, to see the Jews as the devotees, the transmitters, and perhaps even the leaders of world Communism. At the same time, in Russia and in other countries of the Soviet bloc, the Jews were accused and persecuted because they were capitalists, the devotees and leaders of world capitalism.

Similarly, in certain places the Jews were, and to some extent still are, accused of being rootless, without any connection to a people or nation (a quality known as "cosmopolitanism" in the Soviet writing of the time), and in other places they were accused of excessive nationalism and chauvinism, even if it was Jewish nationalism.

The essential flaw in these accusations or contradictory definitions is in their generality. There certainly were certain Jews who were faithful and heartfelt devotees of the Communist movement, just as there have been Jewish capitalists, supporters and adherents of the capitalist ideology. The error lies in making a deduction from a specific detail, or from certain particulars, to the whole.

⟶ Stereotypes in Conflict ⟵

As a general rule, it may be said that the existence of contradictory definitions of the same thing is not a proof that there is no basis for such matters, but rather that each contains only a specific and partial truth and cannot serve as a generalization, as an all-inclusive definition. The source of such erroneous generalizations is sometimes simply a lack of knowledge.

When a person does not know and is not familiar with the whole picture, he tends to generalize on the basis of the few examples that he sees before him. He assumes that it is not just among those particular examples that a certain quality exists but that it is possible to deduce from them a global generalization, which, of course, is meaningless. Moreover, there are cases in which such generalizations are made with evil intent. That is, people knowingly seize on details that are not characteristic and represent them as examples of the whole.

Because the Jews have been nearly everywhere, and have always been a scattered minority in the countries where they resided, they have earned a wealth of definitions, either those that were given in good faith or those that were of an accusing and vilifying nature. Not only are these definitions incompatible, but they very often contradict each other. Even though the people of Israel are autarchic in many spiritual aspects—that is, they live within and for themselves and do not need the definitions or perceptions of others—they have not disregarded such matters, whether they are expressed simply as statements or spoken critically, or even out of hate.

The Jewish response to outsiders' critiques is sometimes agreement and sometimes total opposition. There have been observations that even the Jews were aware of among themselves (traits of character, ways of behaving, gestures, and so on) and even things that Jews were unaware of, or did not deal with—until they were pointed out by some outside perspective that gave a different view of their actions and behavior.

⟶ Excitability and Other So-Called ⟵
Jewish Characteristics

One of the traits often attributed to Jews is their emotional volatility. Different people in different parts of the world think that Jews are too emotional, that they become excited too easily by things that other people do not pay attention to, and, moreover, that they exhibit this emotion in public, both in words and in actions.

On the other hand, others believe that Jews are actually endowed with too much intellectualism or excessive coldness. These people claim that in contrast with those who get excited, express their feelings, and act under the influence of their emotions, the Jews are calculating and cold, and are generally rational, and their actions—perhaps even their thoughts—are logically constructed without taking into account matters of the heart.

These contradictory definitions are not necessarily wrong in principle, since the viewpoint of the other depends to a great extent, for every person and everywhere, on presuppositions that derive from the cultural stance of the observer. There are cultures whose fundamental psychological structure is reserved and cold. In such places it is not only unacceptable to display emotions in public, but too much emotionalism is considered a cultural imperfection. In such a culture of restraint and of inward and outward coolness, a person whose origin and culture are different will be thought of as suffering from excessive emotionalism, as expressing too much emotion. And of course, the opposite is also true: in a culture built on the expression of emotion, a culture in which great importance is given to emotionalism and outbursts of emotion are treated with respect, those who come from other cultures and behave differently seem to be too cold and composed.

It should be remembered that in nearly every place, Jews are influenced to a great extent by their cultural environment and are assimilated in one way or another. Even those whose lifestyles are seemingly isolated and detached from their surroundings are still enormously influenced by their environment and, often, come to resemble it. For this reason, the points of difference, and especially those that are associated with character traits and relationships, can indicate a much deeper inward difference that is not just the result of geographic or cultural distance.

How Can We Be Both Emotional and Intellectual?

It is not surprising, therefore, that Jews who live in different societies and cultures should seem to be too emotional or too intellectual to the people who surround them. However, even when we try to weigh in the balance the local cultural stance in comparison with the Jews, it turns out that the very sense in which Jews are excessive at both extremes—emotionalism and intellectualism—is not only culture-dependent, but has some objective reality, as far as these things can be measured. For example, what seems in certain places to be expressions of cold intellectualism can actually be expressions of something else: a lack of inward identification with various aspects of the society in which the Jews are living.

This lack of identification can derive from various cultural factors. For example, sometimes the Jew is born within a religious-cultural frame of mind that is contrary to or accepts different spiritual assumptions from those of the surrounding culture. In every society, even in a secular one, there are many components that have originated in and are based on elements of a certain religion. These things are absorbed—not particularly in a conscious manner, as part of clearly belonging to that religion, but as part of the residue left by that religion in all aspects of life. As a result, a certain sensitivity is felt toward specific names, images, manners of expression, and so on, which are totally dependent upon some kind of religious experience or background. Therefore, the Jews, and not only those who have a strong religious awareness, but also those who do not, are strangers, to some extent, to these aspects of culture.

The Jewish child who has no Christian background, and who has never visited a church, not even as a purely social visit without any religious significance, does not identify with the basic cultural components of a Christian society, and sometimes even consciously rejects them. Although he might try and even succeed in understanding the culture in which he lives, and can understand the relationships that other people have to certain words, images, and monuments, he cannot attain the same measure of emotional identification. Any response he might have would be necessarily restrained, and even alienated, toward those phenomena. In the eyes of the beholder, this attitude might seem to be coldness, as excessive reliance on reason and intellectualism.

There are other cultural expressions that are not directly associated with religion, but are related to Jewish culture, and because of this they are found at a deeper level in the psyche. Examples of this are hunting and bullfighting. Jews throughout the generations have not only avoided engaging in these kinds of sport, but for cultural reasons they have totally rejected them. When Jews live in a society in which such a sport exists, they may perhaps understand that other people can find pleasure in such things, but it is difficult for the Jews to reach a level of identification with them. They may participate in or watch such a sport, but they will show an emotional distance from that which excites and thrills others.

This phenomenon is present in larger cultural contexts, and it is sometimes described by a Yiddish expression that can hardly be translated and that has been used by the Jews of Western Europe, *goyim-nachas*. This expression is a general definition of things that a surrounding nation enjoyed, such as certain amusements, games, and carousing, which were altogether remote for Jews, not specifically for religious reasons, but often because they were alien to the Jews' inner feelings.

Whenever Jews watched or were involved in a group that engaged in such things, even if there was no aftertaste of disgust or denial, there was a spiritual and emotional distance that could not be bridged. And the non-Jews tended, of course, to interpret this as a lack of emotion, as intellectualism that fails to understand emotional matters when they have no useful value. But this interpretation is not valid, because it is not coldness or lack of emotionalism on the part of the Jews, but mainly the Jewish unfamiliarity with this type of action and attitude.

The same kind of cultural difference can, of course, be seen also as excessive emotionalism, and for the very same reasons. Every normal person has emotions, and moreover whenever the emotional part of the person becomes strong and even overpowering, that person exposes his emotional impulses publicly. In the words of the sages, "A person is known through his pocket [money concerns], his cup [wine drinking], and his anger [emotions]." People do express their strong feelings, each one in the sphere in which he is especially sensitive. There are people whose emotions are aroused by money, whether it is being gained or lost; there are those who become emotional especially while drinking; and there are those whose anger can rise to the level of terrible outbursts of rage. Similarly, people are known by their loves, by the things that they care for and are attached to; in those spheres that they consider to be significant, they experience very strong emotional reactions; and in accordance with their culture and their level of ability to restrain themselves, they also display these experiences outwardly.

However, it is understood that these attachments are not equal for all people. For example, a Jewish value that seems to be found among Jews who are not even aware of their own culture is the high value placed upon life. Certainly, the wish to live is not solely a Jewish one, but the high esteem given to life, in every form and all its manifestations, is a matter of culture, and is rooted in a basic theological perception. The Torah has already identified life with the good, and death with the bad; God himself is called "the living God"; and death and the dead, in spite of the high esteem in which they are held, are considered unclean.

Martyrology has a wider and longer history among Jews than in any other culture. The readiness to die for the sanctification of God's name is also a religious value, a matter that should be focused on during prayer time, and is a subject that is related to the very definition of Jewishness. Nevertheless, the basic perception of the world—in the language of the Psalmist—is that "the dead praise not the Lord." This idea is expressed in far stronger terms in the words of Ecclesiastes, "a living dog is better than a dead lion." Moreover, this perception is part of the inner cultural texture of a Jew. Since a Jew does not seek death in any form whatsoever, not even for crowning glory, his sensitivity to life is much greater, and his conscious and unconscious esteem for it goes much deeper.

It is not surprising, therefore, that Jews react with far greater emotion to the events of life, both to the various stages in the cycle of life such as birth and weddings, and, on the other hand, to death. From this emotional furor comes the stubborn grasp on life, the sensitivity to preserving health, the fear of illness. All these things, of course, are vividly expressed, occasionally are displayed, and even burst out before the public gaze.

Because such an esteem for life and its events does not exist everywhere, and because in many places illness and death are considered less important and less relevant, the Jew appears to be—with his fears, his earnestness, his excitement over all such events—far more emotional than his non-Jewish counterpart. These cultural differences therefore cause Jews to be perceived as both more intellectual and more emotional than those around them, while in actual fact, because of the cultural difference, or because of a different perspective, they react to things in a different way than do the people surrounding them.

The Jewish Love Affair with Words

There is another factor, no less fundamental, that is a common denominator of these two seemingly contradictory phenomena of emotionalism and intellectualism that differentiates the Jews. This common denominator is found in another character trait that is also based upon a deeper cultural essence transmitted from one generation to the other in various ways. It is the ability to think in language.

That is to say, this common denominator is the ability of Jews to express themselves in words, and the ability to refer to these words and understand them in a more skilled way than others. There are cultures and peoples in which thought is mainly visual; their people absorb and relate to pictures, colors, and space. Among other peoples the style of thinking is related to musical sensitivities, to the note and tone of things, to whatever is heard. The high status of words has been an inherent feature of Jewish culture since its inception.

In the Bible, the world is created through ten utterances of God. The first thing revealed is the word of God, and this spoken word is the basis for the whole Jewish culture. The Torah is also the word or phrases from the Ten Commandments to the last verse. Furthermore, even though the Torah demands and activates aspects of faith, love, and fear, and much more as well—the actual carrying out of the commandments concerning great and small things—a central place in Judaism is reserved for the study of the Torah. Torah study is not a technical instrument aimed at teaching what to do and how to do things, but is an aim and objective in itself. As expressed in the blessing on the study of the Torah, this study is to "be engaged in the words of the Torah," which means engagement, thought, repeating and studying the holy word.

Jewish culture is based on words, on verbal concepts that are combined with each other, on the value they have in constructing thought and, no less so, in constructing emotions. From this comes the great Jewish ability of verbal expression and of verbal perception. The sensitivity toward the word and the verbal concept of thought leads to a clearer and sharper way of thinking. Phenomena that cannot be expressed by the mind in a manner that is clear and lucid cannot influence a person's thought processes and reactions.

The Combination of Emotionalism and Intellectualism Is Praiseworthy

Because the Jews have a quality of mind that quickly grasps a word or concept, their reactions to such things are sharper and to some extent more extreme. Words that carry an emotional charge will carry a higher charge for the Jew. Emotions do not remain like a muffled flow within thought, but are clear and sharp, and therefore can be revealed. Similarly, for the same reason, when a thought deals with concepts and rational ideas, it will also be more intellectually developed.

What appear to be two extremes that contradict each other can therefore be understood as two expressions of the same power. Excellent verbal perception, whether it is emotional in nature or rational and utilitarian, sharpens experiences and gives them expression in a most extreme form.

The emotional-experiential side is generally perceived as the polar opposite of the intellectual-rational side. There is indeed a wide gap between the world of emotion and the world of intellect; their paths and activities are very different, and they face in different directions, even if these directions are not necessarily opposite ones. But Jewish experience over the ages has even seen the combination of the two as praiseworthy, and has seen that it should be encouraged and strengthened.

⌒ Prayer and Torah Study ⌒

In traditional terms, the combination of intellect and emotion is expressed in the relation between Torah and prayer. Prayer is, basically, an expression of religious emotion, in all the many ways that it is manifested, in songs of praise, in petitions, in requests for pardon, or in feelings of awe. All these are meant not only for ceremonial utterance, but for the inwardly directed experience that should be above and beyond the words arranged in the prayer book. On the other hand, the study of the Torah is fundamentally a totally rational study as expressed to a greater degree in the deeper and more demanding Talmudic scholarship.

In every generation, of course, some people have tended more toward the emotional side, and have engaged in prayer and in haggadic lore. By contrast, there have also been those who engaged more in Torah study and halachic rulings. But these divisions were not meant to be total and absolute divisions between those who dealt with only one aspect of Judaism or another; there was no Jewish view that only one aspect was sufficient for maintaining a Jewish life. In fact, the rule was that everyone had to be present—and as much as possible steeped—in both these worlds. Naturally, both of them could not be engaged in at the same time, but they could exist compatibly in the same person.

This model has been fostered in all generations, and because of this both sides are a part of Jewish culture and integral to the Jewish character. The feeling that this combination is not only possible but desirable is what produced the combination, which has existed for many generations of outstanding halachic authorities steeped in the metaphysical world of mysticism.

Not every person, of course, can reach the level of such magnificent figures. But this double demand is a normative and general one, and therefore has a comprehensive cultural influence. It is recognized not only in those who attain especially high achievements, but also in ordinary people who, by observing these superb examples, and by recognizing more or less clearly the demands made on the entire people of Israel, are finally able to become a human being that includes these seeming oppositions.

This combination of seemingly both excessive emotionalism and intellectualism is in itself a real combination. Whether people of other cultures understand such a combination and treat it with respect, or whether they feel discomfort or even repugnance toward one of these components, it appears that they are still entrenched in the soul of the Jew and will continue to be so as long as his character remains fundamentally the same.

Questions and Answers

Q *You've discussed how significant both prayer and Torah study are, but most Jews today don't pray or study Torah. How serious do you think that is for our future?*

Rabbi Adin Steinsaltz (RS) Those individuals who don't pray, don't study, and have children who go on like this, will eventually disappear from the Jewish people. It may be that the non-Jewish world will delay this as it has on several occasions. But you cannot take a cat and cut off its head and legs, and then claim that it's a nice-looking cat.

Q *What is Torah study? I suppose that if a person is sitting and study-ing the Talmud one would say that the person is studying Torah. Let's say that the passage the person is studying has a mathematical element. Let's say that there's a mathematician working on the same type of problem but with a textbook, not an open Talmud. Is that mathe-matician also learning Torah?*

RS Basically, no. It's a matter of context. The matter of context, of the framework, is important. To illustrate this, let's say I am making a red dot. I take a brush and paint and make a red dot. Am I an artist? The answer is that if I put it within a picture in the right place, I am an artist. If I put it on a shelf, it may be a marker. If I put it on someone's face, I may be a Hindu. And in some other places, I may just be smearing it.

Q *So what's unique about the context?*

RS By its very definition, it is not only the subject matter of the study. Religiously speaking, study has a dual function. One is that you have to know what the subjects are all about. The other is that study is in many ways a communion. Doing mathematics is not a communion even if you are doing the same thing. Eating a wafer is not participating in a Catholic mass. I myself eat lots of wafers without ever doing so. It is the same with drinking wine. The point is the connection and the communion. If there is no con-nection, there is no communion. That is the point of studying Torah. One part is the context; the other is the very act of doing it.

A part of it is what you know about and a part is the fact that you participate.

Q *And what about prayer? What is prayer? How do you pray to a God you can't know?*

RS That is the problem, the difficulty, and the power of prayer. The basic point of prayer is saying, "I am here. Hello. I wanted to say hello." That is the essence of prayer. It is like a phone call. I make a phone call and say "Hello, I am here." Now sometimes I say something more: "Please, I need a helping hand." Sometimes I say, "Look. I'm really at a tough point." Or sometimes I say, "I wish you would share the view with me." Well, this is prayer. This is the basis of prayer. All the rest is just how to put it into words.

Q *Do we really think that we can change God's mind about something when we pray? Why would somebody have the notion that if I ask the Creator of the Universe, that the Almighty might change the course of things? On a certain level, it seems like a foolish assumption.*

RS It's not a foolish assumption. First of all, I have to express what I wish. It doesn't always mean that my wishes will be granted. You see, when people complain that prayer is not answered, I say that prayer is like using a credit card. You put it in the slot. Sometimes, it is not accepted and the inscription reads "insufficient funds." So this is something that people should remember. I'm asking for all kinds of things, and the answer is often "Your account does not cover it." That is one part of it. People don't like to hear it, especially as a lot of prayers are like this one: "Please give me a loan. I know that I have nothing. Treat me with charity."

But it is important to remember that when I mistakenly think of the Master of the Universe as being the big boss in a company, then I mistakenly conclude that of course the big boss will consult only with the top people in the company. This, in a way, is belittling God, not making Him greater. It is belittling Him because you confine Him, and you make Him like the boss of a company. Being omnipotent and omnipresent means that the difference between a galaxy and my bellyache doesn't have any meaning.

Q *I can understand that in relation to the Infinite there's no difference between me and the Grand Canyon in terms of size. That still doesn't explain why I would be able to change God's mind.*

RS In a prayer, I'm not forcing God; I'm asking for something. I'm expressing my need. Sometimes, if you have a child who gets an allowance, and then the child asks for it at the wrong time, you may say, "No, I made a rule." But you may say, "OK, you're asking. You seem to be desperate." It's a taking into account of my need, and an expression of my need. I'm asking for mercy. I'm saying, "Please, I just need an extra thing today."

Q *Are you saying that my asking for it makes a difference?*

RS It makes a difference, as other things do. I may ask for more money, health, or success. I am asking and sometimes I'm beloved enough to get a bit of mercy.

Q *So it's not enough for me to need it; you're saying that God wants me to ask for it.*

RS He wants me to ask for it because I may need it, and that is also part of the calculation. How much do I feel the need for it? My asking is also a way of expressing a relationship, and of saying, "I don't deny the rules, but I'm asking for a special favor."

Q *But if God knows what was, is, and will be, if God knows my needs before I know my needs . . .*

RS Yes, that goes into higher theology. Then comes, "What is the sense of my doing anything when He knows all?" So in a way He allows the world to pretend it's moving by itself. Belief in free will, which is a strange belief, is that God is creating a world in which He says that some beings have free will and therefore are not just working under compulsion. It's a special arrangement for this particular existence.

Chapter VIII

Why Are Our People Involved in Idolatry?

Our Theocentric Nature and
Our Temptation to Create
and Worship Idols

Different societies have their own physical characteristics, languages, ways of life, and styles of dress—and they also have their own set of psychological qualities. Naturally, as with all other generalities, each nation also has exceptions to the rules, to which such general definitions do not apply. Nevertheless, there is a certain overall structure common to many ethnic and racial groups that distinguishes them from the rest by the presence or emphasis of certain inner qualities.

We could discuss at length the question of whether these qualities stem from education, that is, by the influence of a certain culture that is transmitted from parent to child, or from the environment. It may also be that the matter is a far deeper hereditary structure, and that every construct within that group contains to some degree not only inherited bodily characteristics but also definitive psychological traits.

We all recognize that there are special qualities associated with certain peoples or ethnic groups. In fact, people nearly always ascribe defined characteristics, which often become stereotypes, to other nations or groups.

However, this is not merely a matter of viewpoint or external observation, but also of inward perception. There is hardly any national or ethnic group that has not also laid claim both to certain mental qualities and to all the external components that differentiate them from other groups.

A Trait Can Be Positive or Negative

Like external stereotypes, the inward attribution can be correct or incorrect, more positive or more negative. Sometimes they reflect, inimically or sympathetically, a certain reality, and sometimes a combination of circumstances that have no general significance.

These components may be hereditary or environmental, but they do actually exist.

The evaluation of these qualities depends to a great extent on the observer—that is to say, the extent to which he sympathizes with or is hostile to that group of people. The very same quality that from one perspective can be defined as wisdom or sharpness of intellect may be perceived from another as slyness and duplicity. Similarly, courage and heroism can also be interpreted as stupidity, cruelty, and bloodthirstiness, and so on.

However, the positive or negative evaluation of certain inner qualities does not only depend on the viewpoint of the observer. To a great extent it is also dependent on the use that people make of those inner qualities. All qualities and mental attributes may be positive or negative depending on the situation and conditions in which they appear. The same quality can be positive and excellent within one set of conditions, and harmful—either for the person himself or for others—within another.

Moreover, it may be assumed that the ambivalence found in various psychological traits also takes different forms. Each character trait can have many facets, and its channeling into a positive or a negative route depends to a great degree on the will and choice of the person who has that trait. In certain circumstances, and with suitable effort, a negative character trait can become a positive factor and the opposite can also be true: a character trait that is basically positive might regress—either because of its relations with external factors or because it is combined with other character traits—and reach a state in which it becomes a negative factor.

To illustrate this, the Jewish people are, in many respects, incomparably complex. Yet there are certain traits of character that are apparently more essential to the Jews as a whole and therefore also apply to the individuals that compose it. Among these traits are wonderful qualities that cannot be found anywhere else, and there are also inferior attributes.

～ The Jewish Inclination ～
Toward Idolatry

One of the special things about the Jews is a certain mental quality that undoubtedly exists in other nations, but is more predominant among us, and this is the inclination toward idolatry.

It is not easy to define idolatry, because this term applies to a broad range of things. At a certain level, perhaps the lowest of all, idolatry is simply the cult of objects, of gods made of wood and stone, fetishism that turns into belief. But idolatry is not merely a crude and simple cultic ritual.

It is true that in the Torah and much more so in the Prophets, especially in the Book of Isaiah, war is waged against idolatry mainly in this sense of the word. Yet it should be remembered that during that period an attack against idolatry was not conducted in some large theoretical arena, but was a human and emotional war, against a strange cult, waged in relation to the practical forms that it took. Moreover, because this was an ideological war against idolatry, the attack was not focused on the more crude and materialistic aspects of it that could easily be turned into subjects of satire and caricature.

Idolatry need not be a cult of tangible idols. It can also be the cult of natural forces and objects such as the sun and moon or the sea; there can even be a cult of completely abstract entities that are perceived in the minds of believers not as material forms but as spiritual and abstract images. At times, idolatry represents as gods those entities that are morally reprehensible. In various creeds there were cults of gods who symbolized power, war, sex, death, and so on. Yet even if the entity is not a negative one in itself, and even if it is a totally abstract spiritual entity, the focus on it can still be defined as idolatry.

In the more general sense, idolatry is not specifically the presence of real and concrete statues, or as the multiplicity of gods, but the creation of what the Bible calls "other gods"—that is, the turning of some entity, as it were, into a supreme goal, into a god. This is the most abstract and superior aspect of idolatry. But this, like the material cult of idols, is in complete contradiction to the essential faith in one God.

⟶ The First Jewish Sin Was Idolatry ⟵

The first grave sin, which is the archetype for all the sins of Israel throughout the generations, was the making of the golden calf. This means that the first sin of Israel was idolatry. The fact is repeated over and over in the words of the prophets. With all the variations in prophetic relevance, with all the different emphases on this or that deviation of the people from the right way, there is one common theme among all of them: the matter of idolatry. This is the central subject that occupies all the prophets of the First Temple period, the behavior for which they chastise the people most of all.

However, at the beginning of the Second Temple period, it seems that this idolatrous temptation was totally removed from the Jewish world. The later sages even express occasional wonder at the strong hold this impulse had over Israel in earlier generations. But in fact, even at this later time, this very same inclination was still active, in the Jewish community, since even in those generations there were groups within the people—sometimes very significant portions of it—that left Judaism and turned to idolatry.

For the Hellenic Jew, idolatry was not always practiced for its own sake but rather to become assimilated, to be accepted. The many sects that were formed, the different Gnostic religions that sprang up—all these were powerful factors for generations. The Jewish leadership invested great effort in the war against idolatrous worship, either by physical annihilation (as was done against Hellenism), or by excommunication and public banning from the Jewish community (as was done against the sectarian religions).

Thus, even when it seemed that idolatry was no longer a significant danger for the people of Israel, the inclination and the temptation did not decrease. The growing hold exerted by Judaism on those who remained "inside," as well as the total rejection of all those who could not retain their faith, has preserved the purity of the Jewish core from such temptations.

But the inclination to idolatry still exists in the Jewish people. Sometimes, when the hold of Orthodox Judaism weakens, the urge even among practicing Jews breaks out and rises, and becomes an idolatry that conforms to the times. In other instances, the idolatrous desire causes Jews to abandon Judaism and cling to a new religion, in whatever form it takes.

This bent toward idolatry is not only expressed by the fact that Jews leave their religion and go over to believing in one of some other kind, and not just by the fact that together with a certain retention of Judaism they also hold on to some other, idolatrous cult. This type of idolatry is extremely serious, but the inclination toward idolatry is a deeper and more internal matter.

It expresses not only the hold—both in belief and in cultic practice—of some kind of god, but also a greater devotion in self-commitment and self-sacrifice toward such gods. The Jew who practices idolatry does so not only as a customary habit, according to learned doctrine. He devotes his whole soul, all his powers, to this cult. He clings to it with devotion, loyalty, and self-sacrifice.

⟶ The Other Side of Faith ⟵

The essential nature of this inclination toward idolatry, toward the desire for it and the devotion to it, can be understood as the other side, the dark side, of the basic characteristic of the people of Israel, the power of faith that it possesses. Israel, as our sages say, is a nation of "believers who are the sons of believers." The people of Israel is essentially a people that has not only a hold on its religion, but a very deep spiritual need, a very basic one, for faith. For the people of Israel, faith is not an ornament or a certain part of the scheme of life, but a decisive element that in certain senses is the pivot and center of life as a whole.

Jews are, in essence, in their fundamental quality, a theocentric people, a people for which God and the relationship to God, faith, and religion are a basic need of life, a primary one. For the Jewish people and for the individuals that compose it, faith, devotion, and ritual are not merely something that exists in their world, but a necessity that is derived from their very being.

The force of this belief, this huge religious urge, which has been the basis for the Jewish existence through our long and torturous history, can also deteriorate. Instead of clinging to the faith in God, the Jew may turn all his power of belief, all the resources of his devotion of spirit, and all this mighty thirst to be united with God and to serve Him, in the direction of other aims. Wherever and whenever he transfers his burden of belief to other things, he does so with the same devotion and commitment, with a perfect heart, and with all his might. This is the opposite side, the dark counterpart of the power of belief, devotion of spirit, and commitment to God.

Although idolatry is considered, and justifiably so, to be the total opposite, a reversal of the values of Judaism—and the Sages of Israel have even said that whoever believes in idols is an apostate against the entire Torah—the fact is that both of them, faith and idolatry, have a common source. The very same factor that raises a Jew to a high degree of pure faith is the same factor that drags him into the abyss of idolatry when it becomes disrupted and broken.

As for the various evil impulses, we understand more or less what causes them. There are many urges, such as hunger or sex, toward which a person's body, because it exists as a living being, is propelled. And there are other lures for which the realities of the world impose their demands, such as power, money, and honor. Among all these, idolatry seems like an impulse of no consequence, something that has no justification. The prophets have many words of rebuke for what might be called the absurdity of idolatry: its existence, its ideology, and its external forms. They also wonder at this very substitution, in which a Jew would exchange his love for God and his relationship to Him for the various types of idolatry that exist in his lifetime.

Even though idolatry has no justification, it still has an explanation, and this explanation is found in the enormous difficulty of being a Jew. There are periods in which the difficulty lies in being persecuted, mocked, and humiliated. But in another and more internal way, it lies in the heavy burden of the Torah and its commandments. The Torah is not simply a matter of performing the occasional and limited rituals, but penetrates and influences every segment and sector of life. Add to this the difficulty of isolation, of standing alone, even when it does not involve persecution: the feeling of standing different and alien in front of the entire world.

A Seemingly Impossible Notion of God

Beyond all these burdens, there is the basic difficulty derived from the very belief in God. Belief in God includes from the start, beginning with the Ten Commandments, two components that everyone finds difficult to grasp and to identify with. The first is the perception of God as the One and Only, who is therefore all-embracing and all-supreme, divine, above all comprehension, and therefore far above any personal relationship to something defined and specific. To this is compounded another difficulty, which is a faith that is entirely an abstraction, which does not allow any image, form, or other experience that can be grasped.

Idolatry—in all its forms and at all its levels—destroys this unity and replaces it with entities, whether few or many, that can all be defined and grasped. In contrast, the unified whole that is above the heavens is a concept that is difficult to understand in any form whatsoever.

The idol, whatever it might be, is defined in a way that can be apprehended and perceived. Even when the idolatrous experience is not material and concrete, even when it is an abstract idea—such as love, power, or death—this idea is still a single, simple, and mainly unequivocal thing, which can be grasped by the heart and mind of a person. On the other hand, the unified whole of an entity that is above and beyond comprehension is infinitely distant, and therefore infinitely difficult to conceive of and to identify with.

Another aspect of this difficulty of abstraction is the most basic prohibition against creating a statue or image. The statue or image, the fetish, has an enormous advantage from the emotional viewpoint. It is a thing that a person, at nearly any level, can relate to. Something that can be imagined as a concrete structure, that can be seen, sensed, touched, is capable of realization and closeness. The god that has a specific definition, that takes a human form—the image of a man, his desires—seems far closer and simpler, and can be loved in a concrete and sensual manner.

In a literal sense, the sin of the golden calf is not an apostasy against any specific divine essence, but is an attempt of simple people to give some kind of form to the divine image, with which they could then develop a closer and more concrete kind of relationship. The temptation to identify with and serve something that can be understood, recognized, and to some extent felt and sensed, is very great.

The prophets protested against the preoccupation with sacrifices even in the Temple, as opposed to inward religious commitment, not because they were opposed to the sacrifices, but because this worship became more and more a focal point in itself. They detach one from the perception of divinity and become a relationship to something materialistic—even though they be holy—and they become more and more detached from inward devotion.

The evil inclination of idolatry is thus the outcome of a conflict between the deep need for religion, faith, and serving God, and the human difficulty of creating a relationship with an abstraction. This conflict, this tension, is what creates the temptation to satisfy the longing for the divine with something perverse—that is, by means of idolatry, cultic ritual, and devotion to something simpler and easier for human beings. It is thus that the urge toward faith takes the form of idolatry.

Sometimes when a person finds that the existing forms do not suit him any longer, the urge is to create a new god, a new faith. The Midrash has already said that quite often, when a gentile sees a new type of god that he has never seen before, he says, "This is a Jewish god." That is to say, they see another god that the Jews have created for themselves in order to satisfy their desire and inclination to serve them.

⁓ The Great Spiritual Thirst of Jews ⁓

This idolatrous inclination is the answer to the question of why so many Jews have been drawn to various faiths and religions, and why even in our generation, a large number of them, sometimes even more than 50 percent of believers, in new religions and new cults are Jews. The power of desire and faith has not lessened, and it therefore seeks and finds for itself a twisted pathway of devotion to cults, beliefs, and idolatries of all kinds and forms.

These new religions to which Jews are devoted do not always define themselves as religious movements. The urge toward idolatry can also take the form of secular or even atheist movements and ideologies. In pseudoreligious movements, such as Communism, as well as in many other spheres of religious devotion—in national movements and even in the aesthetic sphere, above and beyond any personal matter or interest—we can also find a religious element, the need to attain devotion, identification, and cultic ritual. Therefore, those Jews who follow such movements do so as an expression of their deep religious nature.

Of course, the evil inclination to idolatry can exist in everyone. But it exists more forcefully in those Jews who are detached, often willingly, and mainly as a result of assimilation, from their own sources. The person who has not received any preparation or followed any significant pathway to reach his Judaism, with all the challenges that it involves, finds himself, in the spiritual sense, in a tough situation. On the one hand, being a Jew, he feels a deep need to identify with religious faith, an inward necessity for religion and cultic ritual. At the same time, the Jewish religion seems strange and incomprehensible to him, and the path toward it is difficult.

For this reason he is impelled to seize on some god, old or new, that is at hand. The inward capacity for faith, devotion, and self-sacrifice is present within him and cries out for resolution, but he himself is misguided, or his parents have not laid out any spiritual guidelines for his personal development, and therefore he seeks and even creates the paths to fulfill his own deep inner longings.

This substitute experience of idolatry is sometimes inadequate and unsatisfying because by his very essential nature the Jew belongs to another world. Yet within this twisted pathway he has nearly no other way to go. As opposed to the evil inclination of idolatry, only a full Jewish life, in practice and in thought, can bring salvation to such a person's soul.

⌒ Questions and Answers ⌒

Q *You once wrote that the Talmud is a photograph of a fountain. When the student of Talmud forgets that and thinks the frozen Talmud is not alive like a fountain that flows, is that a form of idolatry?*

Rabbi Adin Steinsaltz (RS) That is not a form of idolatry; it's a form of misunderstanding. The study of Talmud is a flow in which I ask, I answer, I develop it. If I don't ask, I don't answer; I just see the frozen picture. It's not idolatry; it's just not seeing what it is in there.

Q *Perhaps it is idolatry because it's taking something alive and killing it.*

RS Yes, but killing things is not idolatry.

Q *What, then, are some modern examples of idolatry?*

RS Everything in the street. Money, power, politics.

Q *But money by definition is not idolatry; idolatry is having a certain relationship to money.*

RS The sun and moon are not idols. They become idols when I worship them. Money is itself not an idol; women are not idols. When I worship them, they become idols. Some of the objects that are becoming idols are put on a high theological level. There is a story of Rabbi Nachman in which he shows that honor becomes an idol and death becomes an idol. He speaks about physical fitness, a very modern idea. It can become an idol. The point is that you exercise every day. You exercise constantly. "I lost two pounds," and so on. At a certain point it stops being connected to whatever utility it has and is done for its own sake.

Q *When a person wakes up in the morning and it's the first thing he or she thinks of: "I'm going to the gym."*

RS "I'm going to the gym." Why? It's not that I feel I need exercise. It's not that I can't climb a staircase because I'm too fat. Exercise can and does become an idol. When something that has a purpose becomes an end, it becomes an idol. Sometimes it becomes a big idol around which all my life is centered. Sometimes it's just a middle-sized idol. I'm giving some homage to it, but I also have others. Most people, unless they are really devotees of some kind of thing, are really polytheists. They have a group of idols. As they say in the Talmud, "An idol can be anything from the archangel Michael to an earthworm."

Q *Can the Torah be an idol?*

RS It can become an idol when you separate it from the notion that it is a way to God, a way to practice, when you take it in itself. You can become an idol worshipper of anything. There may be ugly idols and beautiful idols. Even idol worship has different levels.

Chapter IX

What Is Our Role in the World?

Our "Chosen" Status Demands That We Be the Priests to the World

What is the inner nature of the Jew? It appears that the most complete definition of the essential Jewishness can be found in the words that were spoken close to the time when the Torah was given. These words have great importance because they outline the great purposes, the all-embracing principles.

"And now, if you will hearken to my voice and keep my covenant, then you will be to me a special people of all the nations, for all the earth is mine. And you shall be to me a kingdom of priests and a holy nation; these are the words that you shall say to the children of Israel" (Exodus 19:5–6).

These words were an introduction to the general nature of Judaism before the transmission of the details. The reply of the people to these words was as follows: "And all the people answered together, and said: All that God has spoken we shall do" (ibid. v.8). This is a decisive answer, the inward acceptance that precedes all the commandments that came afterward in the Ten Commandments and in the whole Torah that followed.

⁓ "A Special People" ⁓ with More Responsibilities

Three elements are mentioned in these verses, and all of them join together in defining the inner essence of the people of Israel. The first definition is "a special people." This term has been given many interpretations. In a certain sense this is the definition of a chosen people, the acceptance of which is accompanied by a feeling of superiority and sometimes one of pride, but is also perceived negatively by those who see it as an attitude of self-importance.

However, the basic meaning of "a special people" is in fact "a unique people." This uniqueness, the placing of a certain group of people in a role, in a place, in some form of commitment, has an effect on this group, as it affects the individual who attains any level of uniqueness. It implies various aspects of elevation, and even of pride in the special role, in the special status.

But this uniqueness has another facet, no less significant, which is expressed in the sharpest manner by the Prophet Amos (3:2): "You only have I known of all the families of the earth; therefore I will punish you for all your iniquities." The status of being chosen is not only a matter of rights or of a higher standing, but also of duties associated with this special status, which derive from it and perhaps even precede it.

Being singled out in every way means not only being recognized as different from others, but also being the object of criticism that is much more severe. This severe criticism does not necessarily come from the envious and the haters: God himself says that the very status of being chosen demands greater and special attention. Many things that might be overlooked in others cannot remain unmentioned and unnoticed when they concern a person who has the special status of being chosen.

In addition, there is another, more comprehensive significance for a special people. Choice and uniqueness mean being separate, different, and to a great extent also alone, or isolated. The acceptance of this loneliness, even if it is the loneliness of the peak, is difficult.

Individuals, like nations, do not always want to be in a state of isolation. Particular people will sometimes go to any lengths to stand out in a crowd, to be different; however, they still want this difference to be no more than a label—some mark of recognition, but not a cause for isolation. But to be in a constant state of uniqueness means to be alone, as the prophet of the nations,

Balaam, says of us: "[T]hey are a people who dwell alone and are not reckoned among the nations" (Numbers 23:9).

This loneliness has many practical outcomes. People in general cannot and do not even want to protect or guard those who are alone. To be alone also engenders a sense of strangeness, and sometimes even of hate, that derives from the inability of the chosen person to become integrated within the general stream of things—an inability that is not necessarily based on some inward difficulty or problem, but is the result of the choice itself.

Pagan anti-Semitism—and there have been examples of this phenomenon in the Greco-Roman world—was focused especially on this issue of separateness, of the otherness of the Jews, who were not fully integrated into the surrounding society. All the other details, both correct and incorrect, that have been added to this accusation are merely attempts to define the basic sense of public discomfort with those who, in spite of the prevalence of a uniform culture, live in it without merging into it completely, and maintain their particularity everywhere and in all circumstances.

A Kingdom of Priests as Our Primary Purpose

The second condition required for general acceptance of Judaism is to be "a kingdom of priests." The people of Israel is outside the framework of the other nations, since its existence is unlike that of any nation whose justification for existence is its being alive. Any kind of national entity can have various objectives, either for its existence or for the various activities it performs. The main thing is that it exists in and for itself. To be a kingdom of priests means that the people of Israel, as a nation, accepts the role of serving God in the world, or, as the prophet Isaiah says, being "the witnesses" of God (Isaiah 43:12 ff.).

In other words, these are people whose general national purpose is to be the bearers of God's name in the world. Yet being engaged in serving God is not merely a part—whether important or unimportant—of their lives, but is the very aim of the nation's existence, whereas all the other components of its existence are trivial in comparison.

In a nation such as this, the Temple of God is not simply a center for the religious activities of the people, but is the very center of its life, the only thing that justifies its existence. This is the role of the priest: to be the servant of God. The priest is someone whose very essence is his priesthood, and his religious life is his main activity.

Of course, even a kingdom of priests, if it is a kingdom, requires all the other things that any state and nation would need for its existence: it requires work, family and social life, and even war. But all these functions, even if they take up most of the kingdom's resources and time, are insignificant by comparison with the main purpose: to be priests serving God. The entire people thus becomes a single priestly order with a specific aim for its reality, its function, and its very existence—to be priests.

However, we are not describing the social structure of a nation. A specific nation can have a democratic regime, or be led by a religious group, or have any other type of government. But all these are always external matters, additions, some sort of superposition over the basic culture. Jewish existence can also be conducted in various ways, such as anarchy, aristocracy, democracy, or a monarchy headed by a king who is not a priest and does not have the role of a priest. However, not only is the essential nature of government a "nullification of the Torah," but both the regime structure and commercial and social occupations are trivialities compared to the main function—to be priests.

Within this conception of a kingdom of priests, another ideal is embedded. In general, a priest is part of a wider society.

The Jewish people, the "kingdom of priests," are the priests of the world, of all humanity. The priest does not fulfill his function only for himself, but as the representative of others, and he has a certain role within the whole system. Just as in every nation there are priests whose main role and purpose are to be the servants of God, to worship Him, to deliver His words to the people, and to be their representatives to God, so too does the people of Israel have a role in the world: to be the priests of the world, as the Prophet Isaiah says: "And you shall be named the Priests of the Lord, and be called the Ministers of God" (Isaiah 61:6).

This conception, described in the Book of Isaiah as universal, naturally corresponds to an ideal situation, belonging in part to the messianic times to come, when the world will recognize the Jewish role and destiny. However, the function of the priest is not the result of being chosen by others to be a priest, but comes from his essential nature as a servant of God. The task is performed, to a certain extent, in the name of all the others—either in an ideal situation in which they admit that they are in need of it, or when they are unaware of it altogether. The holy task of the priest is based first and foremost on his own awareness that he is bound to serve in that role, and that his whole existence is only to realize this aim.

This concept applies also to the people of Israel. Because it is a kingdom of priests, it is therefore a people that carries the message of God. The entire people, including each person in it, is a representative and emissary of God in the world. For this reason, when the Jew fails in his task or discredits himself in the eyes of others, he is not only slighting himself personally, but also defaming his role, and thus also defaming God's name in the world. When a Jew performs an immoral act—and the more he is identified with his Jewishness, the greater is the significance of his act—he engages in a serious transgression that the sages call a sacrilege.

On the other hand, when he sanctifies the name of God by performing acts of greatness, he does not do it for individual or national honor, but for the honor of God Himself. This idea, which is expressed in the Torah, and in a sharper way in the Book of Ezekiel, identifies the Jewish people as the priests of God and also as the representatives of God because they carry His name, and His name is associated with them. A "kingdom of priests" is therefore the kingdom, the nation, that is nothing except its function of being priests.

⟳ "A Holy Nation" ⟲
Including Everybody

The third condition of the covenant is to be a "holy nation," and this too has a number of different meanings that combine into a single whole. The existence of a "holy nation" means that this role of world priesthood is not the role of particular people within the nation, but of the entire Jewish people, with all its members great or small.

This means the individual cannot say that the priesthood does not interest him, that it is not his business and does not belong to his occupation. A "holy nation" means a whole people that is completely holy, and that is entirely destined for holiness, and each of its parts has a role to play in this framework.

However, even within the people of Israel there is a subdivision of priests who have ritual, cultic functions, of sages who teach others or strive harder in this direction. Yet those with special roles do not exempt themselves from the rest of their duty and commitment. The acceptance of a special role—whether it is inherited or is the result of choice or personal talent—does not free people from fulfilling their duty.

This internal hierarchy is a secondary division of roles within the general framework, and is aimed at the same objectives. Just as the High Priest does not exempt the other priests from their priestly responsibilities, and army commanders and officers do not exempt the rest of the soldiers from their fighting duties, so those who have special duties do not exempt the others from their obligations.

For this reason there did not, and could not, exist a formal group of religious functionaries among the people of Israel who had a status of their own. Undoubtedly, there were, and are, such functionaries, but they do not in any way constitute a separate group because the priestly duties are the general duties of all the people. Those who are exemplary in their service of God are simply a model for others who need to do as they do and to follow them closely.

However, the leadership that has existed for generations— the sages and their disciples—is not a closed group but one essentially aimed at and committed to continual growth. Even if in reality there are Jews, whether few or many, who are unaware of their duties or are incapable of fulfilling them completely, their behavior is considered a deviation, an inability to do the right things, or at the most a temporary situation. The role of priest is not one for particular individuals who are God's servants. This is the task of the "holy nation," the entire people, who are totally directed toward sacred matters.

This holy nation also has another aspect. A priest, as priest, fulfills cultic roles. Whether he offers sacrifices in the Temple or takes on other ritual and sacred roles, these are associated with cultic acts. However, the definition "holy nation" excludes the cultic context, because a "holy nation" includes Jews as well as the whole system of life. A holy nation is one that not only deals, to a small or great degree, with cultic acts; rather, all its actions, everything that it does, must bear the seal of holiness and be performed in the framework of holiness.

Indeed, the system of commandments in Judaism refers only in part to what can be specifically termed a religious cult. Even though the commandments are all associated in some way with religious service, most of them do not do so directly. The majority of the prohibitions and the practical commandments are directed at the general course of life. They lay down guidelines of holiness not only for the way in which to pray or to conduct cultic rites, but also for the entire way of living in all its details.

For example, the commandments dictate how to behave when one wakens from sleep and when one goes to bed, when one is eating or working, in economic negotiations or in war; what food is suitable or unsuitable, what is proper in sexual relations. To be a "holy nation" is therefore not only to adhere to a certain standard of holiness; it interpenetrates with all parts of life, the general and the particular, for every member of the nation.

In an ancient metaphor, which we have already mentioned, in the Book of Exodus, the people of Israel are called "the hosts of God" and "the army of God." The duty of a soldier lies not necessarily in the obliteration of the privacy of his own independent personality, but rather in the submission of all his actions, his way of life, from beginning to end, to the framework of discipline, which gives him one final purpose: to serve all the functions imposed on him as a member of the army, so long as he serves in it. The entire range of commandments in Judaism is an expression of this comprehensive perception of the role.

A Covenant with All the People, Collectively and Individually

Therefore, the conditions prior to the giving of the Torah constitute a general framework. It is the agreement in principle for the Jewish role and destiny, and all the numerous details that follow explain and define how we are to carry out this role. When there is a general readiness to serve, the details and their realization are merely the direct outcome of this agreement and acceptance.

The words of the covenant are addressed to all the people of Israel; they include the community, the kingdom, the nation. The great work that must be done in the name of God for the whole world is a task that only an entire people, focused on it, can fulfill completely. However, not all these definitions apply to the national system. Each term has, for its part, a meaning and implications for the life of every individual, in every role that he fulfills and wherever he is found. Moreover, the special role of "a kingdom of priests" and "a holy nation" cannot be carried out by action of the general public unless all the people who compose it not only cooperate in the action, but are partners in the purpose itself.

Furthermore, just as the "kingdom of priests" has no existence unless it is composed of priests, so also the "holy nation" can only be a combination of individuals, with each of them desiring and striving to be holy. Therefore, the significance of all this is primarily directed toward the individuals, the particulars that make up the whole.

For this reason, it is just that when this covenant was received that no lecture was given before a group of leaders to obtain their agreement, but rather "all the people" were addressed and answered together. This means that the entire people, with all its individual members, had to be a partner in these matters so that the national task could be meaningful.

The Holy Burden

The sages tell us that when we become a holy people and a nation of priests, we accepted "the burden of the kingdom of heaven." This expression shows that accepting the sovereignty of heaven is not a matter of uttering a watchword or expressing enthusiasm. On the contrary, even an agreement in principle means the acceptance of a burden that is not at all easy or comfortable.

According to the sages, accepting the burden of the kingdom of heaven precedes, both in time and in essence, accepting the burden of the commandments. Accepting this burden means—even for each individual—accepting difference and otherness, agreeing to be special. Although this special quality may give a person a sense of superiority, it also commits him to prepare for the solitude that derives from this choice, from the fact that at all times and in every way that he tries to act, he will be essentially different, other, strange to the world. And this choice also includes the mission of priesthood: the main purpose and task for the individual and for the nation is to serve God.

An individual may perhaps not be devoted entirely or mostly to this role as priest and it may be that the course of his life and his limitations will lead him in other directions. However, in the final stage, the choice is what determines the way in which life values are defined, and it is that which makes this value of serving God not a trivial purpose but the main purpose in the life of the individual.

Therefore, the critical question is whether one realizes and fulfills the purpose of his existence or does not do so. Whatever his achievements in other areas may be, if he does not fulfill his main function, he is by definition imperfect; and the more he fulfills it, the greater his success and victory in his path of life.

Naturally, not everyone—and according to a certain definition, no one—can realize this way of life to perfection. But the very sense that this duty is imposed on the individual is in itself part of being a "holy nation." This is not simple or easy. There certainly are individuals who are by nature more attached and closer to it, and perform all these duties in a simplicity of spirit, willingly and by choice. On the other hand, for others, this inner essence of being Jewish is a matter of constant struggle. In such a struggle, there stands on one side the whole world in which the person is at the most merely a collaborator and sometime a total stranger, and on the other side is the person himself, with all his inner hopes and desires, who longs for other things.

It may be that a specific person, many people, and even the greater part of the nation will try to escape from this inner essence, to deny it, or to exchange it—entirely or partially—for other purposes and values. Yet every such attempt at escape and denial, even if it actually succeeds, is a failure from the inner viewpoint. It is a denial not only of the past, of the heritage, or the national duty, however confused it may be, but an escape from the person's essential nature. The changes that are made by everyone are merely masks, disguises, imitations—the exchange of the essential me for other identities. This escape may be successful externally, but it is really a kind of suicide, a denial of the main essence, an escape from the true self.

Questions and Answers

Q *How does a person begin to be a priest? How does that translate into action?*

Rabbi Adin Steinsaltz (RS) The first thing is acknowledging it. Acknowledging it is like being it. "I want to become a priest. I want to be a special servant. It's not enough for me to be one of the flock." That is the first thing. And then, if I am allowed to enter this particular position, there comes a point at which I ask what are the laws, rules, and regulations that priesthood entails. This may be a long study.

Q *How would you react if you heard that a group of people were discovered in the jungle who we've never heard of before, some small tribe,* *and that this tribe tells us that a few thousand years ago, their people received a document from the Creator? And that they believe that they are a kingdom of priests.*

RS Well, we might compare notes, we might even sometimes agree. It will depend then on whether we agree on the nature of the priesthood. A sociologist once said that there are some people whose whole nature is theocentric. His example for this is the Jews—they may not be the only ones, but they are a theocentric people. Their whole existence revolves around God. So in that sense it is not impossible to have a people like this, even though as far as I know none have been discovered.

Q *But if it did happen, would it shake up the foundation?*

RS It wouldn't shake up the foundation. I might believe it or not believe it; I might accept it or not accept it. The fact that there is another claim to anything is not a shakeup. It is not a shock; it is just a trait. If I say that I am so and so and then I find a doppel-gänger, it will be astonishing. Then we'll have to find out who is who and what is what and am I the real person and so on, but that in itself does not make my existence less of an existence. It just means that somebody else has a claim. What I have discussed in this chapter is the notion of the whole people, a notion of a people that is devoting itself to worship, that sees itself as the priests of the world.

Chapter X

How Does Our Jewishness Influence Our Thinking Process?

Marx, Freud, Einstein, and the Jewish Search for Unifying Principles

Many books have been written, mainly by Jews, on the contributions of Jews and Judaism to the civilizations of the world. When these contributions are discussed—both with regard to the number of Jews relative to the world population, and with regard to their essential importance—the results arrived at are undoubtedly most impressive. One may distinguish, however, between those contributions made by Judaism (including the contributions of various individuals who represented the spirit of Judaism and transmitted its contents to the world) and those contributions made by individuals who acted as they did not as Jews but as individual people.

Whether in the natural sciences, in the social sciences, in literature, in art, or in the political and economic life of every nation in which the Jews have been found, the Jewish contribution has undoubtedly been impressive. However, the question should be asked as to the link between this phenomenon and the essential nature of Jewishness.

Those persons who made such important contributions to the world and to its cultures did not do so out of the creative reservoir of the nation as a whole, but as particular individuals, each of whom had a special talent or a highly important idea in one field or another. Moreover, most of those Jews who did important work may have been born Jews, but their perception of themselves, their links to the Jewish people, and even their knowledge of the contents and ideas of the nation were often very slight. The list of the great world personalities who have happened to be Jews might be a source of a certain kind of ethnic pride, but it contains little more than that.

⟶ A Tradition of Learning ⟵

Yet there is another side to this. Judaism as a culture, as a system of opinions and facts, of language and custom, is certainly not inherited. A person cannot—whether genetically or in any other hereditary manner—inherit culture. A child who is the descendant of a multigenerational rabbinic dynasty of great Torah scholars is not born with more knowledge than the son of an ignoramus. Culture and knowledge are acquired through learning, and sometimes even by observation and imitation of surrounding figures.

That is, without learning—conscious or unconscious—these things are not acquired automatically. Elements of knowledge and world outlook cannot be transmitted by inheritance, and they are generally not absorbed except to the extent that there is a high level of knowledge, awareness, and readiness to accept them.

However, there are other aspects that are transmitted from one generation to the other even without the verbal transmission of tradition. Attitudes and approaches, or certain patterns of thought, are not only transmitted from one generation to another, but are passed on even when the descendants do not know, and even if they do not want to know, anything about their collective past.

A person may escape from his country, his birthplace, his family home, and—consciously or by sheer distance—break with all that ties him to his homeland. In the same way, a Jew may distance himself from his cultural heritage and even leave it entirely, sometimes also breaking off all social and family ties. But a person cannot escape from his essential self.

In other words, a Jew may be assimilated, and even be the descendant of several generations of assimilated Jews, but he cannot—even if he is aware of it and wishes it—abandon the basic approaches inherent in him because of the very fact that he is a Jew. These facets are indelible, even when this person is engaged in things that apparently have nothing to do with Jewish culture.

A person can observe anything in the world, either close or distant, but every subject he observes or deals with—whether it is close to the sphere of Jewish culture and affects it, or is detached from it and is even opposed to it—he can only see with Jewish eyes, and he can only think about it with the mind of a Jew.

The Perception of a Unified Essence

In a very general sense, it may be said that Judaism has brought into this world several ideas of great significance: *Monotheism,* directly or indirectly, wherever it is found and has influence in the world, and all that is implied by it or results from it, is derived from Judaism; the idea of the *Sabbath* as a weekly day of rest also derives from Judaism, as does the idea of the *Messiah* as an expectation of redemption in the time to come.

The Jewishness of the Jew finds expression in many and varied ways in the spheres where he is engaged. An example can be found in the widespread influence of Judaism's basic tenet—monotheism, the belief in one God. This belief expresses itself in cultural and scientific works that on the face of it have nothing to do with monotheism, and sometimes even oppose it completely. Certainly, the Jewish monotheistic faith relates to religious matters, to the belief in the existence and unity of God and the perception of the relationship with the divine. But from this belief emerges a perception of a wider world that comprehends all reality, the monistic perception. This implies the assumption that total reality—and every single part of it—has a unified principle, a unified essence, which prescribes its path and through which one may comprehend all that occurs in it.

The monistic perception is more than just seeing a single all-embracing law. It assumes that there is one fundamental principle for the entire aggregate of existence in all its manifestations, and that everything within this aggregate is generated from that basic law. The monistic perception is not in itself a religious perception, and therefore it is not necessarily a Jewish perception. Yet both its details and the way it is approached are linked to a religious perception, not only because of their resemblance and by causal connection.

The belief in one God is not merely an abstract statement about some kind of reality that exists outside of ourselves. It also implies the supremacy of this single essential entity within all reality: all particularities with all their differences and divisions, are unified and subject to a single authority. In this regard, every monistic perception is a kind of comprehensive statement—even if not in religious language—of the very same thing, that is to say, the presupposition of the existence of a unified essence from which the different particularities are constructed and are given significance.

Sometimes the monistic perception is completely unified. That is, it sees everything as emerging from a single point of origin. Sometimes it sees a dichotomous world picture. But even such a dichotomous view is merely a more complex form of the unified perception, because according to this perception a single pair of opposites explains all phenomena. Gnosticism, for example, the dualistic belief in the opposition of the evil materialistic world and the good spiritual world, should be seen merely as a continuation—although a distorted one—of Jewish culture, because its duality of good and evil is, in fact, the continuation of the unified perception in which the Torah is the basis for all understanding of reality.

This unified approach is not necessarily a simple one, and it is certainly not simplistic. No observer can ignore the appearance of multiplicity and differentiation between the particularities of things. But the monistic perception copes with this multiplicity by attempting to combine all phenomena within one basic system, all relating in some way or another to a single unified point.

The deep psychological, intellectual, spiritual, and cultural influence of the belief in one God does not apply only to the religious sphere, or exist in the context of a certain kind of faith. Its outcome—which is a perception that searches for the common factor, the unifying cause, the grand, single, all-embracing principle—exists for every Jew, however distant he may be culturally and consciously from his Jewish origins. There are many examples of this phenomenon throughout Jewish history, both in the internal activities and thought within the Jewish sphere and in whatever Jews have accomplished outside this sphere.

We shall now present a few examples of people and ideas that have created decisive changes in various parts of the world. Although none of these examples are close to anything that is Jewish in nature or is associated with Judaism in any way, still a Jewish essence gives them a certain kind of expression in their formative development.

∽ The Influence of Monotheism ∼ on Karl Marx

One example is the work of Karl Marx. As is known, Karl Marx was a scion of an illustrious Jewish family, but his parents were already totally assimilated and even took care to baptize him when he was very young. Marx's contributions to history, culture, and economics were many, and it may be that a large proportion of them will remain valid even after the grand structure of his creation—called Marxism, and in various places in the world such as in the former Soviet Union, called scientific socialism—no longer has the same decisive influence it has had for so many years. Marx was certainly not the first thinker in the field of economics, nor in the philosophy of history. Even his socialist theories, and more especially his socialist method of thinking, had their forerunners. Yet the enormous impression that his work made during his lifetime, and much more so after his death, comes from building a huge intellectual structure, complex and intricate, based entirely on the tendency to place all phenomena on a single, unified foundation.

Marx searched for a single center around which the whole history of the world, especially world economics, could revolve. In more comprehensive terms, his theories are mainly an attempt to define human history, with all that occurs in it and with all the multiple external factors that appear (events, war and peace, expansion and retreat of nations and powers, as well as human culture and all the achievements of mankind) as the reflection of one problem only, which is basically the problem of economics.

Marx places the whole world on one pillar, on the economic struggle and the direct and indirect influence of economics on every aspect of the world. From this viewpoint, human history and human culture are not a field in which many factors of various kinds are playing, sometimes clashing and sometimes uniting with each other, but the whole of it embodies—even if not always overtly—a single basic motif. The historical and contemporary reality of every culture becomes one system in which all its complex problems are derived, without exception, from one principle.

Marx, like his ancestors, seeks the multiple names and appearances of the phenomena of reality in the reflections of one. This view is in itself neither Jewish nor religious; on the contrary, it is atheistic, and it embodies a certain degree of self-hatred. Although there is no apparent vestige of his Jewishness in Marx, he could not lose this basic component of his worldview: the need to see the world of reality in a unified perspective, deriving from a single source, a single point.

∼ Freud's Theory of ∼ One Fundamental Human Drive

Sigmund Freud had a much closer and more conscious connection with his Jewish world than did Marx, but Freud's world did not contain the basic elements of conscious Jewish culture. The world in which Freud was engaged was a completely different one from that in which Marx had lived: it was a world of the inner mind, the structure of causes that acted within, the ways in which they were manifested, and only to a certain extent—as a kind of superstructure—the more general and social outcome of these things. Here too we find a complicated system that deals with a large number of details and particular problems: dreams, slips of the tongue, neuroses, psychoses, principles of belief and social behavior.

Freud created the huge mechanism, so complicated and mythological, that locates within a person many different parts, various figures and creatures (whose objective existence is certainly doubtful) such as complexes, the id, the superego, and so on. But when one has thoroughly examined all these things, one finds that Freud has built a unified world. In the world of Freud there is, in fact, one working principle, one active significant entity: the libido.

Freud sees the sexual drive as central in a person's life and work. The more he broadens or adds to his method and his understanding of the world, the more he defines all reality in terms of one principle. In this regard, the libido goes beyond the sphere of a certain specific drive that has a certain place and function, and takes on much greater significance. After having erected this central pillar, he tries to build and explain the entire world according to it.

Freud, like his predecessors, uses the ever-expanding method of exegesis. But the material he examines does not consist of written texts; it is reality itself. In looking at experience, the created works of mankind, or the enterprises of society, he stresses the explicit elements, and whatever is not explicit he explicates and interprets in such a way as to link it to the libido. Those elements that seem to contradict his views he explains in some other way until he reaches the same underlying source.

The question of whether, or to what degree, Freud was justified in his conclusions does not concern us here. But it is clear that he has something within him that impels him to think as he does. He is not satisfied with the position that no one else before him has noted. He has a great inner need to present his theory as something that can explain all phenomena, all that occurs in reality. That is to say, a monistic way of thinking, with all its theological implications, is once more revealed in this sphere of thought. Here too the element is not religious at all, and certainly does not derive from Judaism. But this approach, this specific viewpoint, is a clear expression of his Jewish way of thinking.

However, in his later years, it seems that Freud found another central factor in the life of the mind: against the libido he places thanatos. Yet here too he sees these not as two unrelated motifs but as a dichotomy. Eros and thanatos form the pair life and death, creation and destruction, and for this reason these opposites are merely the two extremes of a single unified idea. In this regard, it is interesting to compare the works of two disciples of the Freudian school who broke off from it and built other schools of thought: Adler and Jung.

Jung, who was highly involved in the creative work of Freudian psychoanalysis, broke off and created a world that was not explicitly Freudian. The picture of the world and the mind that he portrayed were composed of various elements that not only could not be found in Freud, but were essentially based on a different approach. Jung does not speak of one component, but rather of many different components, both of human psychological problems and of the more comprehensive outlook of human culture, and does not feel the need to build any unified system of thought that will provide a common factor for all these things.

Adler, who was a Jew, also built a separate system. Although he disagrees with Freud, in principle, like Freud, he describes the life of the mind as built on a single idea, on one factor. According to his view, that essential factor is social stratification, the recognition of personal value as opposed to a sense of inferiority. Like Freud, Adler pointed to a single organizing principle that derives, as we have said, from the essential nature of the creative Jewish person: that drive to find one place, one standpoint, from which to explain reality as a whole.

Einstein's World View Is Basically Theological

This was also the case with Albert Einstein. Although Einstein identified more closely as a Jew than did Marx or Freud, his knowledge and sustenance from Jewish sources was hardly different from theirs. The creative world of Einstein was another world: the physical world of material nature. Yet Einstein's main work—the special and general theories of relativity—is in fact the very opposite of what its name implies.

That is to say, the theory of relativity does not build a relative system in which things are dissociated from each other and are not linked together, but it is a basis for building a more unified system of physics. The "relativity" refers to one dimension in his system of universal determination: the dimension of the speed of light. The relative system that he builds is almost a theological one in all respects. According to it, there is nothing that has any permanent value in itself because everything stands in a relation in which there exists one unified and unchanging entity.

Einstein mainly attempted to reach a unified perception, to find a single common principle. In wider terms, his method was an attempt to combine the dimensions of time and space into one unified concept—spacetime—and to see them as different dimensions of one reality.

A result of Einstein's work is perhaps the inability to see a world that contains elements that seem to exist randomly side by side, are unrelated to each other. For example, Einstein's famous equation, $E = mc^2$, is merely a mathematical expression of this reality that, not by chance, links energy, matter, and the speed of light within a single equation.

In the case of Einstein, the unified perception and the desire to bring all reality back to a single source are not only a matter of theory, but something that Einstein himself well understood. For many years Einstein was obsessed with the attempt—in which he never succeeded—to arrive at a unified field theory, to find the common unifying factor for gravitation and the electromagnetic field. The need to attain such a conclusion underlies the same aspiration that built the theory of relativity, a search for unity.

It seems clear from our examinations of Marx, Freud, and Einstein that the Jewish creative spirit can be far away from Judaism or near it, identified with it or detached from it, and even hostile to it. But the Jew is incapable of escaping it. Because of his essential nature, he cannot see the world in which he is engaged nor the things with which he is concerned, except from the standpoint that Judaism has implanted within him.

∽ Questions and Answers ∾

Q *You write that "Judaism plants in each Jew the unity of all things."
How is this done? Is it a matter of education? Is it somehow embedded
within us?*

Rabbi Adin Steinsaltz (RS) It's very hard to know. The notion of
monotheism has spread beyond the Jews. It is a way of thinking or
a way of behaving that is not completely rational. A person thinks
this way because he's geared to think this way, because he is made
to think along a certain track.

If the trait is genetic, to prove it, the researcher would need
twin subjects. You would have to have one twin who was a Jew and
the other who was a non-Jew and see the similarity between them.
I have a friend, an artist, who claims that he can spot a Jewish artist
anywhere.

But in order to find out about people who do not have the
education and to see how strong the impulse is within them, you
would need several generations in order to check it. I do believe
there is something that is a turn of mind, that is not learned. It's
not just a matter that you are learning that God is one.

Chapter XI

How Does Anti-Semitism Affect Other People?

The Correlation Between a Country's Health and How Well It Treats Its Jews

The famous chapter of Isaiah (53:4–6) that refers to the servant of God reads,

> In truth, he has borne our sicknesses and endured our pains.
> . . . he was wounded for our transgressions, bruised for our
> iniquities. The sufferings were that we might have peace,
> and by his injury we are healed. All we like sheep have gone
> astray, we have turned every one to his own way; and the
> Lord has caused the iniquity of us all to fall upon him.

This chapter is often interpreted, mainly by Christians, as referring to the Messiah. However, most Jewish commentators understand it as not referring to some particular person but as a symbolic reference to the Jewish people as a whole. The people of Israel as a group is the servant of God, that same servant who, while in exile, in suffering, carried the burden of suffering as everyone and for everyone. Although he was despised by all, he was actually the very essence and purpose of everything.

The continuation of this passage in Isaiah proves that the intention is to describe the collective servant of God rather than a particular person, whoever that might be. This is underscored in a very strongly worded phrase in the *Book of the Kuzari* by Rabbi Yehuda Halevi, as a commentary on this chapter and with explicit reference to it. He writes, "Israel exists among the nations like a heart among the limbs."

Israel and the Nations

The problem of the relationship between Israel and the nations is not only a problem of coping with anti-Semitism, or concern over the Jewish position as others see us. In a certain respect, the question of Israel and the nations is not merely one of an external relationship and the attempt to understand this relationship at some level or other. It is also an internal problem. In fact, it is a problem of the significance of Jewish isolation and of hatred toward Israel in all periods of time.

The problem is not a new one, and it did not originate specifically during the period of exile. To some extent it may be said that the problem of the relationship between Israel and the nations has existed as long as the people of Israel itself. Our unique and alien entity is described throughout the Bible and in postbiblical literature.

Let us imagine that the external world is like a mirror that reflects the image of the Jewish people. Throughout its generations, Jews have looked into this mirror and learned things about themselves. This mirror is certainly not always true: it is quite often distorting, but even these distortions can teach us something.

Jews have always been affected by the way the nations see us. Sometimes we deal with it in detail, and sometimes we react to it in silence. But whatever the Jewish reaction to the attitude of the world may be, whether it is an attitude of hatred for hatred, or whether it is expressed in various political ways, it is part of the Jewish experience. It is certainly part of the experience of every Jew as he senses some of this relationship directly and immediately.

We know very little about the relationship between Israel and the nations in the earliest times. We find an attitude of hatred, war breaking out without provocation, and also wars between neighboring countries that have practical explanations, such as fear, desire to conquer, lust for plunder, and so on.

We do not know much about these matters, mainly because we do not have sufficiently good descriptions of how the other nations feel about Israel. But even in the Torah and in the words of the Prophets we are told that the other nations do not see us as just another nation, as a nation that has its own territory although it is still in exile. We are instead seen as unique.

~ "Why Are They Still Here?" ~

In later generations, however, and already in the Second Temple period, we find real anti-Semitism, the anti-Semitism of Greek Alexandria, in which there is a special hatred and enmity towards Jews, who are perceived as a specific and separate entity. The Jews are not a nation like all others with whom one has relationships of dispute or enmity. Instead we are seen as an entity in itself, and the animosity toward it can already be identified as anti-Semitism, in the narrow sense of this concept. From then onward, these relationships have continued to exist down to our own generation.

Anti-Semitism is essentially an ambivalent emotion. Whenever there is a reaction of hatred towards the Jews, and even a demonstration of deep contempt and disdain, these are merely expressions of belittlement. Something that is truly of lesser value is disparaged and contemptible, and no one wishes to deal with it; in fact, it is disregarded and is not discussed at all.

But an anti-Semitic attitude is based on some sort of awareness, willing or involuntary, of a special importance, power, uniqueness, an advantage, which is the cause that arouses the reaction of enmity and hatred. Moreover, anti-Semites generally exaggerate the ability, talents, and aptitude of the Jews. They do so not only for the sake of propaganda or to generate fear, but through recognition, false or true, and through esteem, sometimes even too high an esteem, for the Jewish people.

This ambivalent attitude is more understandable in monotheistic religions. These religions, Christianity and Islam, and all that has emerged and evolved from them, not only were born and grew out of the acceptance (partly or in a fragmentary way) of Jewish ideas, but have been closely involved with Judaism. Their primary, fundamental, and basic perceptions are associated with the Jewish people, and they recognize in one way or another that the Jews were the original chosen people.

This is true not only for Christianity, which takes the Jewish Bible as its foundation stone, and whose central figures and essential character are embedded in Jewish roots, but also for Islam, whose cultural heritage (although not theologically) is at a greater distance from Jewish history. Both these religions recognize that the people of Israel were the chosen people, and that the first revelation of God to the world came through them, through their heritage.

The ambivalence toward the Jews is thus rooted within these religions. On the one hand, they are based on, and depend on, Judaism. On the other hand, they are separated and differentiated from it, almost bound to deny it, to belittle its image, or at least to efface its significance in the present, even if they do not deny its original value in the past.

That there are Jews living today, and that the Jewish faith continues to exist, are painful matters for monotheistic faiths. They claim that the revelations that followed were superior to the earlier ones. That Judaism as a living entity did not disappear when these religions appeared is a problem that does not have any perfect solution.

The attitude toward the Jews was ambivalent from the very start. On the one hand it includes, overtly or covertly, a belief that the Jews were a chosen people—if only in the past—and on the other hand it contains the rejection and denial of Judaism in the present, and, as a result, also of the Jews themselves. In another way, it may be said that the feeling of denial, hatred, or enmity toward the Jews is an expression of disappointed love, of esteem, regard, and attachment, that also contains disappointment that the Jews persist in their existence and continue still to remain apart. And like all unrequited love, it creates a great deal of hatred, or least as much hatred as there was love previous to this disappointment.

There are many other nations that think they possess some distinctive aspect, some mission, and of course some special qualities that cannot be found elsewhere. For example, one thing that is typical of the English is their aversion to the foreigner. The English perceive that everything the foreigner does is of a lower grade, even as they have the sense of mission and duty that comes from feeling that the English serve as a model for the whole world.

This applies to the French sense of intellectual and cultural superiority and to the German claim to be the master race, and to many similar claims. Such pretensions are received by others with disdain or with disregard. At most they become a matter for jokes, but never a subject for all-around hatred.

Being Chosen: Hated If You Are, Damned If You Aren't

In this respect, the self-perception of a people resembles that of individual persons. They praise themselves for qualities that they have or do not have, and consider themselves to be better than others. This becomes a source of enmity only when the outside observer has some reason to think that the claim of being specially chosen has some measure of justification. Then and only then can real enmity and extreme criticism appear.

One who claims to be chosen can become an object of mockery. One who is suspected of being chosen is an object of hatred. For this reason, any Jewish fault, real or imagined, is examined and judged far more than the faults of others. Their deficiencies are treated with leniency, so long as they remain within normal limits, but this leniency is not extended at all toward the Jews.

The individual Jew who steals or cheats will be given greater attention not only because of the enmity toward him, but because there secretly exists a higher estimate, even an exaggerated one, of his advantages and qualities. The greater the estimation of his nature, the greater the stress on his faults, just as a spot on clean clothing is far more noticeable than one on dirty and stained clothing.

In a similar way, nations that are considered barbaric, of an inferior level, and degenerate are described or treated favorably whenever they show some progressive trait that others do not expect to find in them. Among such people, any good action will simply be considered noble, any action that is not completely base will be considered a good deed, and any activity that elsewhere would be normal is considered progressive and viewed as some special advance.

As we have said, the very opposite is true for those who have a sense of being chosen. For them, every descent is a double degradation, every defect stands out and is recognizable to all, and no action that is excused in others is forgiven in them. This double standard is practiced, of course, in the attitude toward the state of Israel. This state is criticized and accused for every deed that is normally condoned in other states.

⤙ Held to a Higher Standard ⤚

The idea that this double standard defines anti-Semitism is an external one. The internal definition is that this standard exists because there is at some level, whether conscious or unconscious, an expectation that Jewish behavior will be far better than the usual norms. Extreme criticism is also a kind of disappointment.

This disappointment, like other human emotions, is certainly mixed with other qualities. There is also some gloating that comes from a recognition of the superiority of the other. Because he is better, richer, more successful, others pay more attention to his defects and weaknesses and emphasize them, often with great pleasure, with that very sense of gloating.

On this point there is a strange coincidence between the external denunciations and the internal words of rebuke. Even the prophet who rebukes Israel, and the sages throughout the generations, have adopted the same perspective with regard to Jewish election, which demands that the Jew be both different and far better than others. The prophet Amos says, "You only have I known among all the families of the earth: therefore I will punish you for all your iniquities" (Amos 3:2).

∼ An Extremely ∼ Vulnerable Minority

During the last two millennia and more, most Jews have lived as minorities in other nations. Every minority living in another country suffers to some degree from the hatred directed at foreigners.

But the Jews were not merely foreigners; they were special in two ways. On the one hand, the Jews were far more vulnerable to all forms of aggression, whether toward them as individuals or toward them as a community. Minorities living in a foreign land generally have a homeland that they can count on. Frequently this support is not strong enough to serve as protection against hatred and persecution, or because of the distance or preoccupation, the homeland cannot defend all its subjects in other countries. Nevertheless, in almost all instances of minority persecution, there is a certain restraint for fear of retaliation or severe punishment that might come from the homeland. But the Jews generally have had no such support, and for that reason they were always more vulnerable than the members of other nations.

The other factor that affects the treatment of the Jews is their separateness, their being so different from all others. A member of a minority group who resembles and acts like the local population is not always instantly recognized, and even an entire community may not be noticeable, and therefore it does not always arouse a feeling of foreignness. But the Jews are foreign and different everywhere, whether in places where they are recognizable even from a racially external aspect, or in places where they stand out because they do not belong to the general structure of the state and the people among whom they live.

This separateness exists both in monotheistic states and in polytheistic ones. Such states may contain many religions and many gods, but the Jews are peculiar because they have denied all those other gods, because by nature they cannot completely join any of the other groups. This fact creates in them an aspect of strangeness that cannot be erased, a foreign quality that accompanies them everywhere.

⌒ The Canaries of Civilization ⌒

Both of the above-described reasons are expressed clearly in the very first anti-Semitic text that appears in the Bible, the words in which Haman sums up the situation regarding the Jews: "There is a certain people scattered abroad and dispersed among the people in all the provinces of your kingdom, and their laws are diverse from all people" (Esther, 3:8). The Jews throughout the generations have been more vulnerable in their weakness and separateness, and this separateness has also made the Jews the most sensitive measuring device for much that occurs in the nations they dwell in.

It is no wonder that so many catastrophes that befall nations all over the world are immediately blamed on the Jews. The guilt of the Jews could be linked to any subject in the world, as in the accusations that Jews were subjected to in medieval times for desecrating the holy bread of the Christians, or the accusations against the Falashim in Ethiopia that at night they turn into tiny creatures who devour people.

In all these cases it did not matter whether the accusations had any basis in reality. They were founded on the still-remaining fact that whenever a catastrophe occurs people try to find a culprit, and that culprit is usually someone other than themselves. Jews have been accused of everything, from the troubles of individuals to the great disasters of the world, because they are clearly the other.

Not only is it simpler and easier to place the blame on them because they are other, but because they are vulnerable it is also possible to express these feelings in actions, or at least in words, in a manner that cannot be used with other people. Of course, whenever possible, rational reasons for hatred could be accumulated. A usurer is never liked by the borrower, the person to whom one owes money is not held in affection by the debtor, and the successful person is not popular with his poorer neighbors. But all these are merely supplementary reasons for the essential fact that is their basis: otherness and vulnerability turn their possessor into an object of hatred, whether this is justified or not.

This sensitivity of the Jews to injury explains why they are injured, but it also points to another matter. Just as a sensitive instrument picks up sound before any other instruments that are less finely tuned can do so, just as a sensitive part of the body suffers from every small blow more than other parts that are less sensitive, so do Jews suffer every malady and injury that exists in the world much earlier and more intensely than others around them.

In other words, the very fact that Jews living in a certain place are suffering is a proof that there exists in that place a much deeper problem: the persecution of Jews is a symptom of some other malady. Xenophobia or religious zealotry can, of course, hasten the onset of such phenomena, or direct them specifically at the Jews, and thus the Jews are the first to suffer. However, as we have said, the source of the problem does not lie with the Jews or with the hatred of Jews, but with an internal problem found in that state.

Generally speaking, it may be said that wherever Jews are persecuted or hated, anti-Semitism is merely the primary or external symptom of deeper problems within the state. Sometimes the same problem that created the persecution of the Jews in a certain place is recognized and open to view, and sometimes it is not visible at all and it takes time for it to be seen by others.

In broader terms, it may be said, even for the great powers and states, that the expulsion or mass emigration of Jews creates a drastic reduction in their national status and strength. Even without reference to moral questions of crime and punishment, even when it is possible to disregard the economic and social significance of expulsion or reduction in the status of the Jews, those very causes that lead to the decline or fall of a nation are generally those that, in a more fine and sensitive sense, led to the expulsion of the Jews.

As the Jews Go . . .

So it was, for example, with the decline of Spain at the end of the Middle Ages. This decline came not only as a result of the expulsion of the Jews, who were a highly beneficial, active, and dynamic element within it, and perhaps even filled a vital role in making it a great empire. It was the self-seclusion, the dependence on taking spoils without creating, the confining fanaticism that is not open to innovation, that brought Spain in the first stage to the expulsion of the Jews, and at a later stage to the total decline of the whole empire.

It may also be seen that the permission that was granted by England to the Jews to resettle there during the Commonwealth regime under Oliver Cromwell in the mid-seventeenth century was linked to some extent with England's economic rise as an empire. Here too, the link is not necessarily causal. It may not have been that the Jews caused this country to grow in power, but rather that those very phenomena that paved the way to England's greatness were also those that opened the way for the Jews to return to that nation.

In a less drastic manner, this situation can also be seen in the diminishing status of the Jews in the Ottoman Empire. This decline is nearly parallel to the gradual process by which Turkey was reduced from a mighty power that ruled over large areas of Asia and Africa, and was even a real threat to Central Europe, to a "sick man." Here, too, it was the restriction of initiative, openness, and energetic activity that had at first prevented Jewish personalities, who had held high positions in Turkey during the golden age of the Ottoman Empire, from filling important roles within its administrative system, and it was this that finally led to the country's decline.

This was also the case with the racial madness that struck the Germans during the Hitler period. This insanity was indeed disastrous, mainly for the Jews in Germany and in other countries, but it was also one of the real causes of the fact that, in spite of Germany's enormous power, the war ended in its total collapse.

Thus, the situation of the Jews in the world is a means for measuring the state of the environment that surrounds them. The more they are hated and persecuted, the greater the problems in the society. These can be actual material problems such as economic crises, national crises, plagues, and the like. But they can also be more subtle issues, such as lack of initiative, dimming of mental alertness, rigidity, conservatism that is not open to innovation, and many more.

Of course, the persecution is always an expression of moral degeneration, of an inability to be introspective, of a lack of awareness, of weakness, of an inability to admit guilt, of hatred.

All these are recognizable first and foremost in the attitude toward the Jews, and only afterwards, in a more general way, in what is happening in the outer environment. As the prophet Isaiah says, the servant of the Lord, injured, suffering, and sick, is not suffering because of his sins, but is suffering for the sickness of others. The sicker the others are, the more he actually suffers.

The inward self-examination of the sufferer is a matter for himself, and another problem is to what degree he is elevated and purified by suffering. But what he can do is to act in such a way that his attempt to reform and change has an influence over others as well. This statement does not refer to the function and destiny of the people of Israel to be a light unto the nations or a guide for others. The essential nature of the people of Israel is not in the function that it carries out for others, but in its very own existence.

Yet the stronger and more complete its existence, the more it also creates a light for others. Its main duty is, therefore, to be itself as much as possible. Others, if they have some wisdom, can understand that for their own sake they should help the people of Israel and support it in every way they can. The burning torch does not give light because it wishes to do so. It blazes because that is its existence, that is the way it expresses itself, and by doing so it also gives light to others.

Questions and Answers

Q *You say that anti-Semitism indicates some deeper malady. What can you say about that in relation to the United States?*

Rabbi Adin Steinsaltz (RS) The relative, though surely not complete, absence of anti-Semitism is in some cases an early stage before overt anti-Semitism. But in the United States at present, I believe it shows that the society is healthier, that it can deal with its problems. Other societies encounter challenges and succumb to anti-Semitism.

Q *So you really think the relative lack of anti-Semitism in the United States reflects our relative health.*

RS Yes. Relative, though. The fact is that it could have grown here as anywhere else. There is no special reason. This country has created lots of racism, but it has conquered a great deal of racism. Yet racism remains in many forms because some of these problems here are not actually problems of race but of social structure and social behavior. Freeing the slaves didn't solve the problems of an uneducated and deprived people. But, yes, in a certain way, that the United States has overcome some racism is again a sign of health.

Q *Do you have any sense of what unique elements that are part of American history allowed this?*

RS The United States has, almost from its very inception, been a new experiment. It has had little to do with native communities, but rather has turned its attention to newcomers. It was, from the very beginning, forced to be a pluralistic environment. America began as a multitude of religious communities. That created a certain amount of fanaticism, but it also created a certain amount of self-reflection. America is still, surely in the West, the most religious country. It is not behaving to perfection, but it is a very religious community. It's very conscious about that. It has notions of right and wrong, what to do and what not to do, and so on. If you look at the fight over racism, you see that it was a real fight. When you think about it, one of the major influences was the book *Uncle Tom's Cabin*. The fact that a book, not even a particularly good book, but a very deeply felt book, had such an impact means that people were sensitive to these kinds of things.

Chapter XII

What Will Become of the Jewish People?

A new slogan, a new cry, is being heard throughout the Jewish world: continuity. But what the term *continuity* really implies is a fight for survival, because only when you are on the verge of death do you speak about some kind of continuity. We are an endangered species, close to disappearing. Hence the cry for continuity.

Although we are struggling to survive, the way we are living shows that we are likely to lose this fight. It will not happen overnight; there are still too many of us to suddenly disappear. But as a people, we are on the way out.

⟶ Juggling Numbers ⟵
Will Not Save Us

We know that some people have tried to change the picture by juggling numbers. You can always say, for example, that intermarriage adds people to the Jewish nation. But all in all, this is just a trick. If someone did such juggling in a financial report, he would land in jail.

We speak about continuity and about passing on our Judaism to the next generation. But what is Judaism? In many cases, it is an empty word. It is what we call, in mathematics, a zero group, a notion that contains nothing whatsoever.

Imagine that someone has a document that can open the gates to Heaven. He takes this document and runs with it to the ends of the world. When he finds he is unable to reach Heaven in his lifetime, he gives the document to his children. And his children go on running with it and keeping it safe, generation after generation.

But with time, the words, despite all the beautiful boxes in which the document is safeguarded, are rubbed away. The people who carry the document are no longer able to read it, and it becomes a faded manuscript. Later still, it is reduced to a mere piece of paper, and even this piece of paper starts to rot.

Yet each new generation takes this heritage and tries to pass it on. Eventually, however, the people who carry the empty box that once contained the precious manuscript will discover that they are running very hard and very fast but carrying nothing. And so they will stop running.

In one way or another, this is what is happening to us. The inscription has faded from our lives. Some of us still speak about our "message," but we no longer know what it is. Not only are we ourselves unable to read it: the words have been entirely obliterated. We have only an empty shell, and even this shell is no longer intact. So we go on, but for how long does it make sense to run with such an empty thing? That loss of inner sense is the essence of the problem.

A people cannot just "go on." Individuals can struggle for personal survival, but for a people that knows it has lost, a struggle for survival seems silly. Survival for what? If I am going to lose anyway, if I am going to pass away in a generation, or in two generations (there are all kinds of demographic calculations), why make my own children miserable? After all, my grandchildren will inevitably forget all about Judaism anyway. If you are lacking not just hope for survival, but hope for something greater in the future, you cannot go on fighting. With only a past and no future, you cannot continue.

People also cannot go on living in the past, even if the past was entirely pleasant—and ours was not. You see, the *shtetl*, wherever it was, cannot be recreated. There is no need and no use for it.

For many people, the state of Israel is a vicarious answer for unsolved problems. But you cannot go on living vicariously. I cannot eat for someone else; I cannot sleep for someone else. No one wants me to beget his children for him. I also cannot pray or study for anyone else. Life is something you have to do on your own.

(Parenthetically, don't depend on the state of Israel to save everything. The state of Israel has its own problems as a center of Jewish existence. It is struggling hard to survive in that sense. It is unable, at present, to do much about saving others.)

There are more Jews, of one description or another, living in the United States than anywhere else in the world, about six million people who can claim Jewish ancestors.

All in all, they have done quite well for themselves. But what they have not done is to create a common future. How many of these people of Jewish ancestry have Jewish grandchildren, or can be sure that their grandchildren will be Jewish? That is the real question.

We Can Either Give Up or Create Something New

Jews in the Diaspora have only two choices. Either they can give up, close shop, and say "We are defeated," or they can create a new way, a new hope. If people want to go on, if they have a feeling that there is something in it, if the memory of the half-obliterated document still possesses some compelling power, then the Jewish life in this country must be rebuilt.

Let me say something full of *chutzpah*: there is a need for, a use for, and even a possibility of making this place something like Galut Bavel, the ancient Jewish place of exile in Babylonia. It is possible to create a second center, comparable to, possibly better than, the main center in Israel. But to accomplish this, one has to do much more than survive. If you cannot do it right, if you cannot create something that will be worthwhile spiritually and intellectually, it is not worth doing at all.

Such an effort would require massive change, not just in priorities, but also in the way people want to do things. It means both a different plan and a different way of planning. It means making big changes in what people are interested in and what they invest in. You see, Jewish education is not just for children, but also for the parents and grandparents of those children, so as to ensure that every grandchild of every Jew remains a Jew.

People also have to make changes in their own lives. You cannot be a perpetual salesman. You cannot go on as you have, creating a whole new culture based on the reselling of *shmattes* (rags). You need a new creativity. And a new creativity means a far deeper involvement for a much broader base of people. This is what survival really means. It is a recognition that if you cannot become bigger and better tomorrow, it is senseless to exist today.

The re-creation here of a significant Jewish culture, even if it is different from that of Israel, does not involve measuring the number of doctors, lawyers, and accountants we have. It is not even measuring the number of rabbis who will emerge from America. That is all a small and partial count. Rather, we must ask ourselves, are we contributing to a Jewish heritage in a way that will be remembered ten generations from now? How many people here will feel distinctly and inherently Jewish? And what will their contribution be to the future? This is the true measure.

To do something like this requires an enormous input, far greater than anything done before. Whatever has been done so far was done with a kind of indulgence money. People paid to get rid of the guilt that came from discarding their Jewishness. But if we want to ensure some kind of future—not just survival, but survival with hope—we must make a much larger investment. I am not speaking only about spending money, but about something more painful—an investment of life.

∽ Our Lives and Souls ∽

There is an expression in the United States: "Put your money where your mouth is." Instead I would say people have to put their lives, their souls, where their money is. This is much more difficult.

I would like to conclude not with a note of prophecy, but at least with a note of hope:

There are still enough Jews here. Many of them, even though very estranged from anything Jewish, are nonetheless good people. We have here, all in all, a fair number of individuals who are first-rate. These people can become the foundation for a different, better future.

But we cannot expect this building to construct itself. There can be hope in our future, a promise, something to reach for. If we want to have such a tomorrow—a real tomorrow, and not just a bleak putting off of death for another half generation—it will require a great deal of effort. But although this work is unprecedented, it can be done.

The Author

Born in 1937 to a secular family, Rabbi Adin Steinsaltz is internationally regarded as one of the leading scholars and rabbis of his time. According to *Newsweek*:

> Jewish lore is filled with tales of formidable rabbis. Probably none living today can compare in genius and influence to Adin Steinsaltz, whose extraordinary gifts as scholar, teacher, scientist, writer, mystic and social critic have attracted disciples from all factions of Israeli society.

Rabbi Steinsaltz's formal education includes the study of mathematics at Hebrew University in addition to his rabbinic studies. At the age of 23, he became Israel's youngest high school principal.

Rabbi Steinsaltz then went on to found the Israel Institute for Talmudic Publications. Under its aegis, he has published more than sixty books on the Talmud, Jewish mysticism, religious thought, sociology, historical biography, and philosophy. These books have been translated into Russian, English, French, Portuguese, Swedish, Japanese, and Dutch. His commentary on *Pirkei*

Avot, the Chapters of the Fathers, has been published in Chinese by the National Academy for Social Studies in Beijing.

Rabbi Steinsaltz is best known for his interpretation, commentaries, and translations of the Babylonian Talmud, a monumental task which he began some thirty-one years ago. Thirty-seven of Rabbi Steinsaltz's Hebrew edition of the Talmud have been published; over two million books are in print. The Rabbi expects to complete the project over the next five years.

Since 1989, Random House has published twenty-two volumes of the English edition of the Rabbi's commentary on the Talmud to great critical acclaim.

The Rabbi is also at work on translations into Russian (four volumes to date) published by the Russian Academy of Sciences, French (eight volumes to date), and Spanish (two volumes to date). With these translations, Rabbi Steinsaltz believes that virtually every Jew, anywhere in the world, will have access to this great repository of Jewish tradition and culture.

Deeply involved in the future of the Jews in the former Soviet Union, Rabbi Steinsaltz travels to Russia and the Republics once each month from his home in Jerusalem, helping to reestablish the foundational institutions of Jewish life.

In Israel, Rabbi Steinsaltz is the Dean of the Mekor Chaim network of schools which encompasses kindergarten through high school. The schools are known for their innovative programming, which goes beyond academics to encourage social responsibility through volunteerism and military and national service. In 1999, the Rabbi opened the Yeshiva Gavoha (Academy of Higher Learning). The Academy is accredited as a *yeshivat hesder* and offers an integrated, five-year program of army service and advanced Jewish learning.

In 1988, Rabbi Steinsaltz received the Israel Prize, the country's highest honor. He has been a resident scholar at major academic institutions in Europe and the United States, among them

Yale University, the Institute for Advanced Studies in Princeton, and the Woodrow Wilson Center in Washington, D.C. In 1995, he received the Legion d'Honneur, the French Order of Arts and Letters.

Rabbi Steinsaltz's activities in the United States are supported by the Aleph Society, headquartered in New York City.

The Editor

A leader in the world of Jewish book publishing, Arthur Kurzweil has published over 650 titles of Jewish interest during the last twenty years. For seventeen years he served as editor-in-chief of Jason Aronson Publishers and was, for nearly two decades, the editorial director of The Jewish Book Club. A former president of the Jewish Book Council, he currently serves as Judaica consultant for Jossey-Bass/Wiley Publishers where he is building a new list of important books of Jewish interest.

Arthur Kurzweil is a devoted student of Rabbi Adin Steinsaltz and is the editor of two collections of the Rabbi's writings, *The Strife of the Spirit* and *On Being Free*. Under Rabbi Steinsaltz' direction, he is also the Coordinator of The Talmud Circle Project, an initiative to introduce the study of Talmud to Jews around the United States. Mr. Kurzweil is responsible for the formation of many synagogue groups where the Talmud is studied regularly.

Renowned for his groundbreaking book, *From Generation to Generation: How to Trace Your Jewish Genealogy and Family History*, now in its third edition since first published in 1980, Arthur Kurzweil is also the author of *My Generations: A Course in Jewish*

Family History, which is used as a text book in synagogue schools throughout the United States. He is also the editor of *Best Jewish Writing 2003* (Jossey-Bass/Wiley).

Arthur Kurzweil is the recipient of the Distinguished Humanitarian Award from the Melton Center of Ohio State University for his unique contributions to the field of Jewish education. He also received a Lifetime Achievement Award from the International Association of Jewish Genealogical Societies.

A popular speaker on many subjects including genealogy, Talmud, and Jewish theology, Arthur Kurzweil is also an accomplished magician. He is a member of the International Brotherhood of Magicians and the Society of American Magicians, and frequently performs his one-man, one hundred minute show, "Searching for God in a Magic Shop." In his performance, he accompanies mind-expanding magic with profound philosophical and spiritual ideas. He is the proud father of three children and also shares his life with, at the last count, one parakeet, one parrot, and six finches.

Index

Index

Denial, of essential Jewishness, 152. *See also* Assimilation
Destiny, common, 47–48
Deuteronomy: 9:13, 71; 10:16, 71
Dialogue in Hell Between Montesquieu and Machiavelli (Joly), 19
Diaspora: defining Jewish identity in, 40; future of Jewish people in, 186–188; Hebrew literacy in, 46; individualism and, 72; lack of unified leadership in, 25, 29, 31
Disappointment, 173–174
Disease, demographics and, 63, 64
Dissension. *See* Quarrels
Dissociation, 70–71, 75–76
Double standard, 172–174
Duality, 159

E

East Indians, in United States, 21
Ecclesiastes, 118
Economics, unifying theory of, 160–162
Edomites, 55
Education, Jewish, 187
Egypt: Exodus from, 30; Jewish community in, 29
Einstein, A., 164–165
Elders of Zion, 24–25, 35
Emancipation period, 8
Emotionalism: cultural elements of, 117–119; intellectualism and, 114–126; over life events, 118–119; perception of excessive, 114–126; verbal expression of, 120–121
England: Jews in, 177–178; sense of mission of, 172
Eros, 163
Esau, sons of, 68
Esther 3:8, 175
Ethnic group, Jews as, 47–48
Exegesis, 163
Exercise, 139
Exile status: money-related professions and, 82, 83; population thinning and, 65–67; vulnerability of, 174–175. *See also* Expulsion
Exodus, 30

Exodus, Book of, 149; 32:9, 71; 34:9, 71
Expulsion: as cause of migration, 28; from Jewish community, 91, 132; negative effects of, on nations' status and strength, 177–179. *See also* Exile status
Ezekiel, Book of, 147

F

Factionalism, 34–35, 41. *See also* Quarrels
Faith: idolatry and, 130–131, 133–134; as Jewish character trait, 72–75, 76
Falashim, 176
Family: adoption/conversion to, 53–55, 59–60; assimilation and, 55–57; functional and dysfunctional, 60; Jewish identity as, 48–60; leaving, 53–55, 67–68; loyalty to, 58; nonbiological, 49–50; quarreling within, 57–59, 60; rebellion against Jewishness and, 51–55; religion and, 50–53, 59
Farming, 81–82, 84–85, 86
Father: God as, 50, 51–52; relationship between child and, 50–53. *See also* Patriarchs
Feudalism, 82–84
First Temple period, idolatry in, 131
Flexibility. *See* Adaptability
Ford, H., 19
Fragmentation: factionalism and, 35; from role-playing, 8–10
France, anti-Semitic literature in, 18
Free will, 126
French people, 172
Freud, S., 162–164
Future, of Jewish people, 183–188; in the United States, 186–188

G

Galut Bavel, 186–187
Gaon, H., 26
Gaon, S., 42
Generalizations, 112–113
Genesis: 14:17, 53; 42:12, 56–57
Gentile converts. *See* Converts, gentile-to-Jewish

Index

84; realities of, 21–22, 90–92. *See
also* Money and money dealing
White man's burden, 108
Will to live, 70, 78
Words: emotionalism and, 120–121;
importance of, 119–120
World domination, Jewish: anti-Semitics'
belief in, 18–22; Jewish reality *versus*,
21–37
Writers, Jewish, 23

X
Xenophobia, 177

Y
Yemenite Jews, 47
Yeshivot, 33
Yevamot 27a, 54

Z
Zealotry, 177

HICKMANS